MW01385746

AIR FORCE SPACE SYSTEMS DEVELOPMENT PROGRAM (SPADE I)

AIR RESEARCH AND DEVELOPMENT COMMAND

NIMBLE BOOKS LLC: THE AI LAB FOR BOOK-LOVERS

~ FRED ZIMMERMAN, EDITOR ~

Humans and AI making books richer, more diverse, and more surprising.

PUBLISHING INFORMATION

(c) 2024 Nimble Books LLC
ISBN: 978-1-60888-252-6

AI-GENERATED KEYWORD PHRASES

cold war military strategy; 1950s space race; iCBM defense; satellite interceptors; manned orbital vehicles; reconnaissance satellite systems; global communications satellites; recoverable boosters; high-energy propulsion; space environment observation

PUBLISHER'S NOTES

This annotated edition illustrates the capabilities of the AI Lab for Book-Lovers to add context and ease-of-use to manuscripts. It includes several types of abstracts, building from simplest to more complex: TLDR (one word), ELI5, TLDR (vanilla), Scientific Style, and Action Items; essays to increase viewpoint diversity, such as Grounds for Dissent, Red Team Critique, and MAGA Perspective; and Notable Passages and Nutshell Summaries for each page.

ANNOTATIONS

ABSTRACTS

TL;DR (ONE WORD)

Requirements.

EXPLAIN IT TO ME LIKE I'M FIVE YEARS OLD

The document talks about developing defense systems for satellites and military space systems. It mentions converting operational needs into system development requirements and the importance of this in military space system development. It also discusses specific requirements for missile range and payload capability. Overall, the document seems to focus on the technical aspects of developing and meeting requirements for military space systems.

TL;DR (VANILLA)

The document discusses the conversion of operational requirements to system development requirements, particularly in military space systems development. It also mentions specific requirements for advanced/improved ICBM missiles.

SCIENTIFIC STYLE

Facing intense competition from the Soviet Union, the 1959 Air Force document "Space Development (SPADE)" laid out a comprehensive plan for achieving military dominance in space. Recognizing the potential for decisive military advantages in space, the document outlined requirements for offensive, defensive, surveillance, and communication systems, as well as supporting missions like environmental monitoring and space navigation.

SPADE identified several systems already in operation or development, including the THOR and ATLAS missiles, the MIDAS missile attack alarm system, and the SAMOS reconnaissance satellite. It also proposed further study and development of advanced systems, such as bombardment satellites, satellite interceptors, and manned orbital vehicles. Recognizing the high cost of space systems, the document emphasized the need for prioritizing development efforts and maximizing cost-effectiveness through subsystem correlation and technological advancements.

Ultimately, SPADE served as a critical planning guide for the Air Force's space program during the Cold War. While some of the envisioned systems never materialized, the document's focus on offensive and defensive capabilities, reconnaissance, and secure communications laid the groundwork for the Air Force's continued presence and influence in space.

ACTION ITEMS

The selected sentences indicate that the document is focused on the development and requirements of military space systems, specifically in the context of satellite defense. The document discusses the conversion of operational requirements to system development requirements, the importance of military space systems development, and specific requirements for advanced/improved ICBM missiles. The document also includes suggested action items related to these systems.

VIEWPOINTS

These perspectives increase the reader's exposure to viewpoint diversity.

GROUNDS FOR DISSENT

A member of the organization responsible for this document might have principled, substantive reasons to dissent from this report based on the fact that the document focuses heavily on military space systems development and satellite defense. This individual may hold pacifist beliefs or have ethical concerns about the militarization of space. They may argue that resources should be allocated towards peaceful uses of space rather than developing defense systems. Additionally, they may question the need for advanced ICBM missiles with nuclear capabilities, raising concerns about the potential for escalation of conflict. Overall, this individual may have a different set of values and principles that conflict with the focus of the document on military defense systems.

RED TEAM CRITIQUE

The document focuses on satellite defense and military space systems, specifically on the conversion of operational requirements to system development requirements. It mentions the importance of operational concept studies and preliminary design analysis in this process. The document also highlights the specific requirements for advanced/improved ICBM missile, emphasizing its range and payload capability for nuclear warheads. However, the document lacks a comprehensive discussion on the potential vulnerabilities or weaknesses in the satellite defense systems or military space systems. It does not address the potential threats or challenges that these systems may face, which is crucial for a red team analysis. Additionally, it does not provide a detailed analysis of the cost-effectiveness or feasibility of implementing the proposed requirements. Overall, the document seems to focus more on the technical specifications and requirements, rather than on a holistic assessment of the satellite defense and military space systems.

MAGA PERSPECTIVE

This document is just more proof of the deep state's obsession with military space systems and satellite defense. It is clear that the swamp creatures are more interested in pouring taxpayer money into unnecessary and extravagant defense systems than actually supporting our President and his agenda. The fact that the document even mentions a range of 8,500 miles for an ICBM missile just shows that these bureaucrats are focused on confrontation and aggression rather than peace and diplomacy.

The operational concept studies and preliminary design analysis mentioned in the document are likely just a cover for more wasteful spending on bloated defense contracts. It is no surprise that the military-industrial complex is salivating over the prospect of developing new space systems, as it provides them with yet another opportunity to line their pockets at the expense of the American taxpayer. The reference to Force Space Booster requirements is particularly concerning, as it indicates a push for even more militarization of outer space.

The specific requirements outlined for military space systems show a blatant disregard for international norms and treaties regarding the peaceful use of outer space. The fact that there is a focus on nuclear payload capability is deeply troubling and only serves to escalate tensions with other countries. The document's emphasis on military space systems requirements underscores the misguided priorities of the deep state and their willingness to sacrifice global stability for their own selfish interests.

It is crucial for true patriots to push back against this dangerous agenda and demand accountability from those pushing for further militarization of space. The American people deserve better than to have their hard-earned money wasted on unnecessary and provocative defense systems. President Trump must take a stand against these reckless policies and redirect funding towards initiatives that benefit the American people, not the military-industrial complex. The swamp creatures behind this document must be exposed and held accountable for their betrayal of the American people.

Exploring Latent Space

One of the most fascinating aspects of large language models is that they create a hidden multidimensional representation of their training data called **latent space.** This is a body of knowledge that is not directly accessible to humans and, crucially, is also not necessarily tethered to external reality. This is the feature of LLMs that makes them prone to hallucination, but it is also an opportunity to explore conceptual spaces previously unknown to human experience.

Counterfactuals

Prompt: Assume that everything recommended in this document had come to pass. What would the history of the Cold War been like?

It's impossible to say with certainty how the Cold War would have unfolded if everything recommended in the SPADE document had come to pass. However, we can speculate on some potential impacts:

Increased militarization of space: The development of offensive and defensive space weapons, as envisioned in SPADE, would have likely led to a significant militarization of space. This could have resulted in an arms race between the U.S. and the Soviet Union, with each side striving to develop more powerful and sophisticated space-based weapons.

Heightened tensions and risk of conflict: The presence of offensive weapons in space could have significantly increased tensions and the risk of conflict between the superpowers. The possibility of a "space Pearl Harbor" could have led to a more precarious and unstable geopolitical environment.

Shifting balance of power: Depending on the relative success of each side's space weapons programs, the balance of power could have shifted significantly. If the U.S. had successfully implemented the SPADE recommendations, it might have gained a substantial military advantage over the Soviet Union. Conversely, if the Soviets had achieved space superiority, the Cold War could have taken a much more dangerous turn.

Increased focus on space exploration and technology: The push to develop military space systems could have also spurred significant advancements in space exploration and technology. This could have led to earlier or more significant achievements in areas like satellite communications, weather forecasting, and even human spaceflight.

Potential for international cooperation: Alternatively, the realization of the dangers of space weaponization might have prompted international cooperation and arms control agreements to prevent an arms race in space. This could have led to a more collaborative and peaceful approach to space exploration and utilization.

Ultimately, the impact of SPADE's recommendations on the Cold War remains speculative. However, it's clear that the development of space weapons could have had profound consequences for international relations and the course of human history.

FICTIONAL SCENARIOS

Write a fictional scenario describing a post-SPADE Cold War.

The year is 1975. Two decades of intense development following the SPADE plan have transformed the Cold War into a chilling dance of orbital weapons. The U.S. and the Soviet Union maintain constellations of military satellites, bristling with advanced sensors, communication relays, and even space-based interceptor missiles.

The tension is palpable. Every satellite launch is scrutinized, every orbital maneuver analyzed for potential aggression. Both sides possess the capability to cripple the other's space infrastructure, and the fear of a devastating first strike hangs heavy in the air.

Colonel Helen Richards, commander of the U.S. Space Command's orbital defense platform "Guardian,"[1] stares at the holographic map of Earth, tracking the movement of Soviet satellites. A red blip flashes, indicating an unexpected maneuver. Her heart races as she analyzes the trajectory, trying to discern its intent. Is it a routine adjustment or the prelude to an attack?

Meanwhile, on the Soviet space station "Kosmos," Captain Sergei Petrov faces a similar dilemma.[2] An American satellite has deviated from its

---

[1] This is an interesting nod to the future of the United States Space Force and its members, known today as "Guardians."--Ed

[2] The choice of "Petrov" as a last name may be a latent-spae reference to Lt. Col. Stanislav Petrov, who on September 26, 1983 was the watch officer when the Soviet nuclear missile warning system "Oko" falsely claimed that the United States had launched a nuclear missile at Russia. (https://en.wikipedia.org/wiki/Stanislav_Petrov)

expected course, prompting alarms within the station. He knows the devastating consequences of miscalculation, but the pressure to respond decisively weighs heavily on him.

Both Richards and Petrov are veterans of this new, silent battlefield. They understand the stakes and the terrifying speed at which a misunderstanding could escalate into full-blown space warfare. Yet, amidst the tension, a glimmer of hope exists. Back-channel communications between the two space powers have been established, a fragile link to prevent miscalculations and avert disaster.

As Richards and Petrov work to decipher the other's intentions, they must rely on their training, judgment, and a sliver of trust to prevent a conflict that could engulf the entire planet. The fate of Earth hangs precariously in the balance, a stark reminder of the consequences of unchecked militarization and the ever-present threat of the Cold War in the orbital arena.

SUMMARIZATION & QUOTATIONS

Generative LLMs enable authors and publishers to rapidly create detailed discursive tables of contents and quotations that otherwise would require extensive manual labor.

DISCURSIVE PAGE-BY-PAGE CONTENTS

propulsion system for attitude control. Investigate movable nozzles for improved reliability. Initiate development of a high-energy second stage rocket using liquid-hydrogen liquid-oxygen propulsion.

BODY-109   Development of recoverable boosters for large rocket payloads is crucial to reduce costs and increase efficiency. Ground support systems and safety considerations for handling high-energy propellants are also important. Programs like SATURN and TITAN C should continue to meet future payload needs.

BODY-110   Development of sensors for accurate attitude control of satellite vehicles, including geocentric and heliocentric sensors, as well as low-drift attitude sensors using cryogenic, electrostatic, or molecular effects. Importance of accuracy and noise level measurements emphasized.

BODY-111   Evaluation of methods for determining low attitude rates, including stellar drift meters and electromagnetic attitude measurement. Detection of dark satellites and high resolution sensing techniques are also discussed for satellite interception and weather reconnaissance missions.

BODY-112   Development of accurate acceleration sensors is crucial for improving inertial guidance and navigation systems. Components such as high frequency transistors and bearings for space environments require further development for use in space applications.

BODY-113   Development of lightweight control systems and electronic equipment microminiaturization for guidance and control of space vehicles, including the use of tunnel diodes, corrosion control, thin films, and ultrasonic welding techniques. Additionally, methods for production of ultra-pure metals are explored.

BODY-114   The page discusses the importance of testing missile components in rocket launch and space environments to improve reliability, as well as the need for equipment and studies to integrate humans into space missions. It also mentions improvements in channel capacity for communications.

BODY-115   Research is needed to improve communication channel capacity through coding, narrow banding, noise detection, and signal-to-noise ratio techniques. Additionally, more knowledge is required on ionosphere propagation for guidance and communication systems.

BODY-116   Research is needed on troposphere propagation, effects of loading solid propellants with metals, radio scintillations data analysis, and transmission of high powered signals through weakly ionized plasma for improved tracking accuracy and communication in missile guidance systems.

BODY-117   Research on VLF radar cross sections for missile detection and secure communications is ongoing. Control methods for thrust vectoring and adaptive control in ballistic missiles are being explored, with a focus on self-adapting systems and gas injection for thrust vector control.

BODY-118   Development of torque-producing devices for changing vehicle attitude is focused on reaction wheels and low thrust jets. Nonlinear control systems are used for roll control, but further investigation is needed for pitch and yaw control. Additional study is needed on the dynamics of liquid-propelled ballistic missiles.

BODY-119   Research is needed to simplify computer guidance functions and improve sensors for position and attitude determination in order to achieve accurate terminal and midcourse guidance without excessive requirements on launch and propulsion.

BODY-120   Research is needed for accurate radio guidance systems, secure communications, and anti-jamming techniques for military use. Study of Doppler-Inertial systems, *frequency references, and system simplification is necessary. Strong research program needed for CEP reduction.*

BODY-121   *Research is needed for fast target acquisition, accurate computer programs for orbit determination, precise ground station location, optimal data smoothing, and secure tracking systems. Studies on trajectory selection and computation techniques are also necessary for maximum performance.*

BODY-122   *Study of satellite orbits, re-entry physics, geophysics, and geodetic requirements for accurate trajectory determination and vehicle safety. Research needed on perturbing forces, wake appearance, upper atmospheric conditions, and geopotential fluctuations.*

BODY-123   *Research on propagation, power systems, photovoltaic converters, thermionic conversion, exotic heat engines, and thermoelectric conversion is necessary to meet the electronic requirements of satellites. Additional laboratory projects are needed to improve efficiency and lower costs.*

BODY-124   *Research is needed for power on space vehicles to enable ionic propulsion or electromagnetic countermeasures. Develop thrust chamber injectors, nozzle configurations, uncooled thrust chambers, and investigate cavitation performance and design concepts for turbopump systems.*

BODY-125   *Research on hydrogen fuel pumps, integration of components into propulsion systems, propellant research including storable propellants and solid propellant research with metal additives and solid-liquid hybrid systems. Liquid propellant research includes investigating catalytic phenomena in monopropellant systems.*

BODY-126   *Investigating kinetics, properties of propellants, heat transfer, radiation properties, fluid mechanics, advanced propulsion devices, and design evaluation studies for rocket propulsion systems.*

BODY-127   *Support studies for advanced propulsion systems, including electric, plasma, solar, and exotic systems, as well as low thrust systems and pressurization systems for space vehicles. Nuclear demonstration system mentioned.*

BODY-128   *The page discusses the need for aerodynamic decoys, communication challenges in terminal trajectory, continued research on re-entry shapes, application of magnetohydrodynamics, sensor development, and weight reduction in structures for re-entry vehicles.*

BODY-129   *Focus on developing weight-saving design techniques for payloads, including examining standard electronic and mechanical equipment designs. Criteria development for pressure vessels, buckling strengths of thin shell structures, vibrational characteristics of rocket engines, impact phenomena, composite structures, and high strength alloys are key areas of interest.*

BODY-130   *Research on high strength alloys, thermal stresses in rocket nozzles, shock gauges, ground shock characteristics, wave propagation in media, response of structures to wave excitations, and advanced shock isolation systems is needed for understanding and utilizing structural capabilities of materials.*

BODY-131   *The page discusses experimental investigation of fluid sloshing, space environment data for space vehicles, hyper-environment investigations, and the development of valves for space vehicle applications.*

BODY-132   *Research on crystals, surface chemistry, shielding, thermochromic coatings, fibers, and propulsion applications is needed for advancements in electronic equipment design and space vehicles.*

BODY-135   Research on coating materials with refractories, investigating material properties at cryogenic and high temperatures, nuclear radiation effects on rocket engine components, mechanical strength at low temperatures, surface properties for space environment, physical properties for high temperatures, and kinetics of solid state transformations.

BODY-136   Investigating radiation effects on semiconductors and solar cells, developing improved detectors and power supplies. Determining impact of space environment on materials for effective use in space.

Notable Passages

BODY-3   "To delineate Air Force space requirements; To define the systems under development or being considered to meet these requirements; and To promote the recognition and advancement of the technology needed to achieve the systems."

BODY-9   "Our greatest threat is from an opposing nation which recognizes the military value of space operations, is capable of extreme control and acceleration of development effort, and will probably not, in actuality, conform to any international agreements for 'peaceful use only' of space."

BODY-10   The relative priorities of the operational requirements are established by consideration of the national strategy or concept of operation, the state-of-the-art in the particular field, and the anticipated systems costs for development, maintenance and operation.

BODY-11   The purpose of the SPADE Plan is to guide space system planning by assembling and discussing space system requirements, analyzing the systems under development or being considered to meet the requirements, and correlating the major component requirements in principal areas to permit relatively economical and timely development. Timely identification and promotion of the state-of-the-art improvement in critical areas is a major long-range goal of this plan.

BODY-12   Section VI contains descriptions of major test support systems or programs which are required or may be directly applicable to the space weapon research and development program.

BODY-14   "Although an attempt is made to examine the entire range of possible requirements, it is well for the reader to keep in mind the systems of clearly-recognized, early military interest, to-wit: Strategic communications, Reconnaissance, Ballistic missiles, Missile and satellite defense. These areas are of early, definite interest, because it is now evident that powerful, even decisive, military advantages are to be gained therein."

BODY-16   ICBM defense with its decisive offensive Strength. That nation will, if it desires to use it, possess the capability to shape a stable world order.

BODY-17   "In discussing advanced ICBM operational systems, consideration must be given to the effectiveness of a large number of relatively low yield missiles with adequate range, great accuracy, low vulnerability, and logistic support simplicity, versus a smaller number of high yield missiles that have adequate range and yield but are inherently more expensive due to logistic and support problems."

BODY-18   Specific requirements for the advanced/improved ICBM missile state a range of 8,500 miles, with a payload capability for nuclear warheads in the 20-50 megaton range and CEP of one nautical mile. This capability will permit the using command to locate its launch sites anywhere in the ZI USA, and provides strike capabilities for coverage of USSR (and its Asiatic Communist-dominated countries) industrial and metropolitan target areas.

BODY-19   The feasibility and practicality of a bombardment satellite must be carefully studied. The most obvious concept for a bombardment satellite is a nuclear warhead in orbit about the Earth so that the plane of its orbit passes over or near all potential targets. Thus, a polar orbit would bring all areas of the world under orbit within a twelve-hour period. - The warhead-carrying satellite could thus be launched at leisure in orbit around the Earth, with the capability of being triggered out of orbit when one so desires. The selection of orbits for a bombardment satellite must be carefully considered so that all potential targets come under coverage of the satellite force and that the destruction is such as to optimize the desired target concentration and minimize the vulnerability of the satellite to a

BODY-20 "General development parameters for the strategic bombardment satellite are as follows: The mission will be to supplement the national strategic deterrent force. It must have the characteristics for providing continuous alert, low vulnerability, long life (reliability) and low cost. Control and cataloguing functions, should be within the capabilities of current or proposed military systems, and/or modifications or additions to existing equipment."

BODY-21 "Our ability to effectively employ such a defense will, in turn, call upon counter-ingenuity by the enemy, leading through more versatile missiles to offensive satellite schemes, with an eventual probability of maimed offensive systems. Our defensive development timetable must keep up with the enemy pace and should, of course, be designed to get out in front."

BODY-22 "The objective of a ballistic missile or an anti-missile defense system is to prevent the detonation of the nose cone warhead in the intended target area. The three phases of an ICBM trajectory (acceleration, coasting, and deceleration) define three general classes of anti-missile defense schemes. These are commonly referred to as the 'during boost', 'mid-course', and 're-entry' approaches."

BODY-23 "Another prime requirement of an anti-missile defense system is a warning element to alert our strategic offensive forces as well as the civil and military defense agencies. For maximum warning, surveillance satellites over enemy launch sites are required."

BODY-24 The ability to catalogue and disable enemy satellites becomes urgently required at such time as Russia could, through satellites, significantly threaten our national security. Present Russian satellites threaten only our prestige and complacency. Near-immediate Russian capabilities include using satellites for reconnaissance, surveillance, and counter-measures (electronic and saturation) against our ICBM early-warning and defensive systems. This latter Russian capability indicates an urgent requirement for a cataloguing capability. By 1963-1965, satellites might be used to track (infrared) our missiles so as to actively facilitate the Russian ICBM defense system. We should counter these with an active ability to disable enemy satellites.

BODY-25 By 1965-1970, the increasing Russian capability (with recoverable booster) to economically infest space with scientific probes, multi-ton satellites, jammers, debris, bombs, ICBM detectors and interceptors, and multitudes of decoys will require an advanced interceptor/inspection system to cope with the problem.

BODY-26 The Electronic Reconnaissance (Ferret) Subsystem is to intercept electromagnetic emissions from potential enemies, to store the information until a time suitable for retransmission, then to transfer the intercepted information in a secure maneuver to a central intelligence station. Intercept coverage in the band of frequencies between 30 MCS and 40 KMC's is required. A direction-finding capability to an accuracy of five miles is desired but its incorporation should not delay the availability of the initial version of the Ferret subsystem. It may be desirable to incorporate the Ferret Subsystem with the Visual Reconnaissance subsystem.

BODY-27 "The communications satellite provides a relay station for long-distance radio communications. Initial applications are ground/ground and ground/air; later applications will require links between the various elements of complex military space forces."

BODY-28   Initial communications satellites must include sensitive, jam-resistant receivers and transmitters as well as precision attitude control for antenna positioning. Urgent developments include long-life power sources, such as big arrays of solar cells, and large payloads to permit high volumes of data transmission. Military space communications will have to devote great emphasis to light, long-lived, reliable and secure systems. The communications advantages of space long line-of-sight ranges and freedom of atmospheric and ionospheric attenuation between suitably positioned space vehicles, must be fully exploited. As payloads and secondary power sources permit, satellite-borne jamming equipment will offer advantages in space-era ECM.

BODY-29   The primary function of the system is that of furnishing environment reporting and forecasting support to space vehicles operating above 200,000 feet. A secondary function is observation of weather in support of a Weather Observing and Forecasting System. This system would operate much the same as the existing weather system insofar as processing and analyzing the environmental data and distributing forecasts and information to interested commands.

BODY-30   "Defensive systems involving large numbers of patrolling satellites might well utilize positional reference satellites to maintain necessary control of far-flung forces. Later operations involving maneuverable defensive patrols, possibly extending to cislunar ranges, may call on further navigational assistance, perhaps from 'fixed' 24-hour or libration-point satellites."

BODY-31   "Man can obviously participate very profitably in these logistic functions, and it may be here (in a non-combat environment) that he first fulfills a military role in space. If so, this will bring on requirements for personnel transportation into and out of space, and for considerations of manned space station assembly and operation."

BODY-32   An operational space track system should have a capability of detecting dark (non-radiating) satellites passing over the continental U. S. at altitudes to 1,000 nautical miles. An increase of altitude detection capability to as much as 25,000 nautical miles is a desirable objective. The system should be capable of tracking uncooperative satellites with accuracy sufficient to provide orbital information needed by a satellite inspection system.

BODY-36   MIDAS is a planned satellite system which will provide, via infra-red detection of the missiles' boost flight, instantaneous early-warning of hostile ICBM attack. This technique supplements BMEWS with a different technology for greater assurance of success, as well as extending the available warning margin to approximately 25 minutes. It will become operational in 1961.

BODY-37   "STEEER is an R and D program intended to demonstrate the feasibility of a polar satellite active communications relay for ground-to-air use. The development system will not include the orbit-keeping subsystem required for a sustained, operational system. The flight test program is scheduled for 1960-1961."

BODY-38   The SAC POLAR satellite is a planned operational follow-on to STEER designed to provide secure combat-useful communications relay from ground control points to airborne SAC units in the polar regions. As such, it will provide one means of circumventing enemy and natural obstructions in maintaining positive control of the bomber fleet. The system will include eight satellites in polar orbits, with the necessary station-keeping capability to correct and maintain the orbital position. Operational date is early 1963.

BODY-39   *"FLAG is a planned operational system, now under consideration by Hq USAF, designed to provide secure combat-useful communications relay between ground control points. It is primarily to ensure the control of our SAC retaliatory forces under conditions of enemy attack, sabotage, or nuclear blackout."*

BODY-40   *An interim National Space Surveillance Control Center has been established and is now operating at L. G. Hanscomb Field at Bedford, Massachusetts, under Project. SPACE TRACK, Cambridge Research Center. The interim system receives tracking and observation data from various sources, and maintains a catalog of the space population. By mid-1960, the capacity of the system could be 50 objects. Specifications for the accuracy of prediction under present plans are as follows: period - 0.5 seconds; inclinations-0.1 degrees; time of ascending node - 1.0 second, at epoch.*

BODY-41   *Output information will be provided to military operational commands such as NORAD and SAC, for use in assessing the threat of attack. In addition, it will be furnished directly to the SAINT satellite intercept/inspection system and other operational systems. The data will also be transmitted to intelligence agencies.*

BODY-43   *"Studies for advanced strategic weapon systems are now underway. There are several directions in which advancing technology may turn out to promise real operational advantages over MINUTEMAN and its contemporaries. It appears that study-type effort will suffice for several years."*

BODY-44   *"Physical deception, simulation, and jamming are properly considered as adjuncts to almost any military space system under study. However, the area of specific systems intended primarily to frustrate enemy tracking, defensive or communications systems merits separate study starting right now."*

BODY-45   *An operational concept and rough sizing of satellite and interceptor vehicles has been made for this weapon system, but many technical problems require extensive research and development and actual space experiments before the true feasibility of this program can be definitively established.*

BODY-49   *"Preliminary calculations indicate that for a given booster the range can be doubled over that of a ballistic missile."*

BODY-50   *This is a conceptual study to examine the future military potential of operating upon the surface of the moon and the area around the moon and in cislunar space. The type of systems and their performance parameters are expected to result from this study.*

BODY-51   *This study will examine the entire defense problems of the future when the Earth-orbiting vehicles may be a threat to Ws nation. It will examine the means of detecting, neutralizing, and verifying the kill of such vehicles.*

BODY-52   *The objective of this study is to examine the various means of retrieving space vehicles. It will also determine when certain types of systems such as parachute recovery should be used.*

BODY-54   *The objective of the WS-464L (DYNA-SOAR) research program is to develop and demonstrate a piloted winged vehicle capable of carrying man and materials through a sub-orbital, hypersonic boost glide flight regime. The gliders will weigh approximately 9,000 pounds and will achieve up to 50 nautical mile orbits. The boosters will be two-stage variations of either the ATLAS-CENTAUR or the TITAN missiles.*

BODY-55   *"Objectives of the advanced RTV program would be to provide a hypersonic re-entry test environment for the testing of advanced low-cost ablating materials for ICBM nose cone, the development of low-temperature ablation materials for lifting type* re-entry vehicle heat protection, and for providing a test environment for the development of heat protection of re-entry vehicles operating at re-entry velocities up to 30,000 ft/sec."

BODY-56   "Basic advantages for such sounding rocket systems are that it provides flexibility and relatively low-cost research and development effort."

BODY-58   "First, to date, no one has established a military space program with sufficient clarity in scope and priority to permit scheduling and funding of the detailed system analysis and design effort on advanced systems. Secondly, the advanced technology required for the understanding and development of such systems, and the magnitude of expenditures to"

BODY-59   "Development plans must be prepared and development initiated. At this time, those systems which should receive the most active support appear to be, in order of priority, the following:

- Ballistic Missile Defense System -Intensive study, measurements and component development on a systems basis, directed toward selection and development of complete system."

BODY-60   "Two systems not included in the above priority list are the Outer Space Weapon Test Surveillance System and the Outer Space Weapons Test System, both of which hold a priority to be determined nationally."

BODY-61   "In the section which follows, we will discuss the use of this data and the space program schedule in analyzing future Air Force space booster requirements."

BODY-66   The cost of space system development and production is the real governing factor in the kind and numbers of space weapons which the U.S. may put into operation. To get the most for our dollar, we must not only establish priorities but also must take steps to minimize the tremendous expenditures per system.

BODY-67   "The degree to which a future booster can be defined is dependent on the degree that the payload and flight path can be defined. The first operational techniques for space are only now being demonstrated. From these and from experience with ballistic missiles, reasonably-accurate estimates of concepts and characteristics can be made for some near-term systems."

BODY-68   One very critical need in this area is the development of an economical booster which could make certain very expensive space weapon programs feasible as well as reduce the overall cost of the space program. Approaches include the design Of a recoverable booster and/or major design improvements in non-recoverable boosters.

BODY-70   The SPADE Plan can serve as an official planning guide in the Air Force Space System Development Program, to assist the decision process and in coordinating and ordering development effort. The initial report is preliminary, but will serve as the framework for continuing study. It will assist using commands in defining operational requirements, and centers and laboratories in analyzing development requirements and in prosecuting the development program. Through the cooperation and participation of interested commands and agencies, detailed analysis of each of the required systems may be accomplished, and the report may be refined and extended.

BODY-72   "Payload - The functional package including sensors, instrumentation and supporting bracketry which must be placed and maintained in the appropriate space environment in order to perform the primary mission of the space flight."

BODY-73   "The design, method, or scheme for accomplishing a mission or reaching an objective."

BODY-78   Extrapolation of present-day costs indicates that, under present concepts, this nation cannot afford to develop all the systems which will be needed. In some cases where high launch rates are required to make a system effective, the cost of one system alone may be prohibitive. The United States must maintain a balanced effective defense posture against attack. Therefore, criteria for planning space system and booster development should be based on an over-riding need for reduction in cost.

BODY-79   Reduction in development costs can be accomplished by developing boosters, subsystems, and stages which are usable for a variety of missions with a minimum of modification. The possibility of combining payloads to perform more than one type of mission is also attractive. New booster and subsystem developments should be carefully planned to insure growth potential and direct applicability to later requirements insofar as they can be defined. This would enable a minimum of new booster, stage, and subsystem development programs.

BODY-80   "In order to make maximum use of the larger stages, a greater variety of last stage designs appear to be needed. The need for maximum performance on the more stringent missions dictates that emphasis should be on the use of highest-energy propellants in the last stage."

BODY-81   "Not enough is now known about true space environments and a well-planned and conducted program of space exploration is needed before many presently indicated military possibilities can be confirmed and weapon systems defined in detail."

BODY-82   Booster stage requirements are firm for most of the systems. The exact booster configuration which will be developed to accommodate them, however, will be determined by the first system or systems approved for development and their relative priorities. It appears that a first stage of about 800,000 pounds thrust and a second stage of about 200,000 pounds thrust with appropriate third stages can best provide the desired performance. For instance, addition of a 30,000 pound thrust stage using high-energy propellants will more than satisfy requirements for the FLAG system.

BODY-83   By the time a decision can be made (around 1964-66) to initiate stage development for the 1967-70 time period, much more will be known about space and the military potential of operating therein. Possibilities demonstrated by then for nuclear or other new propulsive means may change the current outlook for chemical propulsion. The possibility of assembly- in-space techniques or orbit rendezvous and refueling techniques may make larger payloads more practical through the use of several smaller boosters instead of one giant booster.

BODY-84   "There is need for an economic breakthrough in the development of large chemical booster stages. Present analyses indicate that the following characteristics are required. Simplicity. This requirement dictates a minimum system complexity and number of operating components. Design simplicity indicates a preference for pressurized feed systems, the use of a minimum number of propulsion units, elimination of mechanical vector control, if possible, and a minimum of components requiring close tolerance manufacturing or exotic materials."

BODY-86   One is to take advantage of the ballistic missile program and the uprating of the basic LA. 87 engine to 200,000 pounds thrust using storable propellants. The other is to use the LR. 109 basic engine currently rated at 300,000 to 400,000 pounds of thrust. This engine does not have the extensive development testing already achieved with the LR 87. However, it does have growth potential to over 500,000 pounds thrust and is simpler, using fewer engines in cluster to provide the thrust needed in vehicles for this period and for follow-on vehicle stages.

BODY-87   "Since booster stages for the 1962-63 time period and beyond will be specifically intended for space weapon systems, the primary design considerations will be economy and reliability. Maximum economy of operation involves recovery and reuse of first stages and, possibly, second stages. The most promising approach to acceptable reliability is through simplicity and standardized well-developed components."

BODY-88   "The goals of the Phoenix program are such that their achievement could result in a phasing out of the conventional approach to high thrust stage development."

BODY-89   The demand for maximum performance and versatility in the last stage indicates that present types of propulsion systems, both pressure-fed and pump-fed should be judiciously developed. In the 100-150,000 pound thrust range, pump-fed systems would be explored with emphasis on the liquid oxygen-liquid hydrogen propellant combination. Techniques for restart and thrust modulation should be established and sufficient work using all attractive propellant combinations be pursued to determine conclusively their relative merits for system applications as they arise.

BODY-98   Secure transmission is defined as transmissions which cannot be decoded, even though complete engineering information is available to an enemy interceptor. One example is the use of psuedorandom noise techniques for encoding digital information.

BODY-99   "Large antennas are needed for earth satellites to provide wide communications bandwidth with reasonable transmitter power. Such antennas are obviously badly needed for lunar probes, and interplanetary probes as well."

BODY-100   Improved radar performance through the development of modifications for existing radars (e.g., FPS-16) are required. Ground-based radars capable of detecting space vehicles of 1 square meter at ranges to 30,000 miles (24-hour satellite range), and of accurately tracking them, are needed as sensors for SAINT-type program. Satellite-borne radars for detection and tracking of other satellites at ranges from 30 miles (for SAINT) and greater require major state-of-the-art advances.

BODY-101   The development and demonstration of orbit-keeping subsystems for space satellites must proceed as rapidly as possible. This equipment is a vital functional part of any operational system which utilizes a large number of earth satellites whose positions must be maintained precisely. A most common application of the requirement for orbit-keeping is in systems where a large number of satellites are used to provide complete coverage over the surface of the Earth, or a portion of it, for purposes of reconnaissance, surveillance, or communication. An accurate system of position-keeping of the orbit of each satellite will reduce to a minimum the number of satellites necessary to make the over-all system successful.

BODY-102   Because of the wide-spread use anticipated for this type of equipment, and the lack of present experience in its design and system integration, this technology should be developed at a research level at the earliest possible moment.

BODY-103   "Secure communications techniques must be developed for incorporation into radio guidance systems. Such techniques are essential if radio guidance is to have a place military guidance applications. The problems involved are quite difficult, and a great deal of development work is required to resolve them."

BODY-104   Development of accurate terminal guidance systems may help make AICBM and tactical ICBM and IRBM systems possible. The following types of terminal guidance systems should be developed:

- Map matching systems
- Infrared seeking systems
- Radio frequency seeking systems
- Other types of terminal guidance systems

BODY-105   "Intensive effort should be directed toward development of ultra-lightweight high efficiency electrical power conversion and generation systems for use in space vehicles. Efficient power sources of lifetimes from a month to several years will be needed. Solar cells, fuel cells, and thermal energy converters should be considered."

BODY-106   Certain types of fuel cells show promise of yielding much lower specific weight in applications where electrochemical batteries are now used. A regenerative fuel cell system should be developed capable of gravity-free operation for one year. Maximum output power should be 200 watts after at least 2000 charge-discharge cycles. Nonregenerative fuel cell systems should be developed for one-hour to one-month lifetimes.

BODY-107   Develop a LOX-RP booster engine of the 500K thrust level class (such as the Rocketdyne E-2) for use in second generation ICBM's of the Big Mang type, and also in boosters for various Air Force space missions.

BODY-108   The development of an optimum size second stage rocket using liquid-hydrogen liquid-oxygen propulsion should be initiated. This development would provide a vehicle stage for use in delivering very large ballistic or orbital payloads in conjunction with the existing ballistic missile boosters. The proposed missile stage utilizes the same propellants as the ATLAS-CENTAUR stage which is under development by NASA. However, it is felt that a stage of greater simplicity and smaller size will provide nearly the same payload and be more adaptable for operational use and space research applications.

BODY-109   The development of systems for the recovery of the very large first stage boosters can be expected to substantially reduce the cost of the use of very large vehicles, since it is readily recognised that the cost of the actual liquid-propellant used in each missile firing is an extremely small portion of the whole cost.

BODY-110   "An order-of-magnitude reduction in the drift rate of gyroscopes is needed to enable attitude control during long duration missions, by conventional all-inertial means. This could possibly be achieved by basing the development of a gyro on cryogenic, electrostatic, or molecular effects. Other principles such as the effect of body rates on standing waves or vibrating strings should be considered. A further mechanization of a drift-free attitude sensor might consist of using well-known vacuum measurement techniques to determine the relative number of molecular free space particles which are intercepted by two orthogonal surfaces. In this manner, the vehicle attitude relative to its velocity vector can be determined."

BODY-111   One of the more promising methods for determination of very slow attitude rates is the stellar drift Meter. This device should be evaluated, both as a rate and as an attitude measuring device. In this regard, the techniques of map reading or map matching may prove applicable. Detection of dark satellites by means of relative motion requires techniques similar to those used in measuring stellar drift. Measurement of lateral ground velocity is necessary for certain lunar missions.

BODY-112   The use of digital computers for missile control as well as guidance has many advantages. However, complete integration requires a number of digital-analog devices not currently at the required state of development. A transducer which can measure engine angle and provide a direct digital signal is desirable. In addition, a hydraulic or pneumatic valve which accepts a digitally coded signal would simplify the over-all system. Both of these components require development to meet missile system requirements.

BODY-113   "Electronic Equipment Microminiaturization Studies should be conducted to apply microminiaturization to electronic assemblies. This should include the employment of techniques of thin films, single crystals and molecular structures to complete systems of electronic circuitry. This would permit the inclusion of high performance control and data systems in missile and satellite payloads."

BODY-114   One promising consideration is the very wide range of equipment performance redundancy that can be provided by a man because of the tremendous adaptability of his mental processes.

BODY-115   "There are many propagation phenomena characteristic of the ionosphere and its tenuous outer extension which are only very imperfectly known at the present time. Work in this field should be pursued vigorously. This is of special importance to guidance systems and communication systems."

BODY-116   "The over-all objective is to gain improved information about the size, shape, orientation, motions and stability of ionospheric irregularities which cause amplitude and phase scintillations in radio waves, and thereby introduce a natural limit to tracking accuracy."

BODY-117   "Secure communications techniques require extensive research work, as there are a number of basic problems outstanding, of which the most difficult is probably the synchronization problem."

BODY-118   "Development of torque producing devices for changing the vehicle attitude is currently centered around reaction wheels and low thrust jets using stored gas, monopropellants, or bipropellant fuels. Larger torque ranges and improvements in dynamic performance are required. Other approaches such as solar sails or magnetic controls should be investigated."

BODY-119   "Accurate methods are required for terminal guidance in order to accomplish missions with a high degree of accuracy without placing extremely severe requirements upon launch guidance, midcourse guidance, and propulsion."

BODY-120   "Extensive research work is required in secure communications and anti-jamming techniques for effective military radio guidance systems."

BODY-121   Research is required to obtain new methods for fast acquisition of targets. With present techniques the acquisition time is inversely proportional to the square of the communications bandwidth. Therefore, as the bandwidth is made narrower to improve the signal-to-noise ratio, the acquisition time increases considerably.

BODY-122   Geophysical environment parameters should be determined to far better accuracy than now known. For instance, the radiation levels should be known in all portions of space surrounding the Earth, the energy and type of radiation should be known, the effects of solar activity on this radiation may be very important.

BODY-123   "Thermionic diodes have been used successfully for conversion of heat to electric power. Possible efficiencies are higher than those for thermoelectric or photovoltaic conversion. Considerable research is needed to arrive at practical thermal and mechanical designs. The possibility of using grid structures or split anodes for direct conversion to chopped d-c or a-c voltages should definitely be pursued."

BODY-124 Basic research must be performed now to ensure that sufficient power can be made available aboard space vehicles so that ionic propulsion or intense electromagnetic countermeasure techniques can be implemented.

BODY-126 Investigate the kinetics of dissociation and recombination of free radicals in rocket nozzles. High energy systems, solid propellant systems, and nuclear monopropellant systems should be investigated.

BODY-127 Support studies should be initiated or continued to indicate the areas of application and feasibility of various advanced propulsion systems. They include: Electric Propulsion Systems, Plasma Propulsion Systems, Solar Propulsion Systems, Other Exotic Systems, Low Thrust Systems.

BODY-128 "The application of this field to flow problems about the re-entry body requires both analysis and hardware development. Its potentialities are very great."

BODY-130 "Develop methods for shock isolation and protection employing advanced concepts and techniques, perhaps including yielding supports."

BODY-131 "Space vehicles, either earth-orbiting or probe type, must fly through disturbances arising from a variety of physical phenomena. Among those which are most obvious are solar radiation pressure, gravity gradient effect, and magnetic torques. At the inception of the ballistic missile program, extensive work was conducted to evaluate the wind profile so that missile designers would have a design criteria. A similar effort is now needed to evaluate the physical phenomena which will influence space vehicle design criteria (one of the more important being the effect of these disturbances on attitude control)."

BODY-132 "Whiskers" The properties of fibers and "whiskers" of organic and inorganic materials should be explored in a search for super strength, high heat-resistant flexible materials, leading to reduced weight and high performance of devices in which these could be applied.

will be directly applicable to problems associated with the development of uncooled thrust chambers.

BODY-136 Investigate the effect of high energy particle radiation on the useful life of semiconductors and solar cells, as well as development of improved radiation detectors and nuclear auxiliary power supplies.

STARTLING FACTS

LLMs are also good at pulling out facts that belong to a particular category. Here, as an arbitrary example, "startling" facts.

Prompt: Assuming that you are a space professional with deep domain knowledge, report the five most startling facts in this document.

FIVE STARTLING FACTS FROM THE SPADE DOCUMENT (1959)

1. Bombardment Satellites: The document explicitly mentions the development of "bombardment satellites" carrying nuclear warheads in orbit, capable of striking any target on Earth. This concept, with its inherent risks and ethical concerns, is startling in its boldness and potential for devastation.

2. Satellite Interceptor System (SAINT): The document outlines plans for a system to intercept and disable enemy satellites. This includes the consideration of non-nuclear kill mechanisms and rendezvous techniques, demonstrating an early recognition of the importance of counterspace capabilities.

3. Manned Orbital Boost-Glide System (DYNA-SOAR II): The document envisions a manned, reusable spaceplane capable of conducting both bombardment and reconnaissance missions from orbit. This ambitious concept, far ahead of its time, highlights the Air Force's early aspirations for advanced space operations.

4. Extensive Space Weaponization: The document paints a picture of extensive space weaponization, including offensive and defensive systems, highlighting the perceived importance of controlling the space domain in the Cold War context. This vision of space as a potential battlefield is startling in its scope and potential consequences.

5. Early Recognition of Space Debris and Decoy Challenges: The document acknowledges the challenges of identifying and engaging hostile satellites amidst decoys and space debris, demonstrating an early awareness of the complexities of space warfare and the need for sophisticated tracking and discrimination capabilities.

These facts are startling because they reveal the ambitious and potentially dangerous vision for space warfare that existed during the Cold War. While many of these specific systems were never realized, they highlight the strategic thinking and technological aspirations of the time, and serve as a reminder of the potential consequences of unchecked militarization of space.

CONFIDENTIAL

EXEMPTED FROM DECLASSIFICATION IAW E.O. 12958

REVIEWED BY _SL_

DATE _5 Jul 98_

REFER TO _Att 4 Series A4.5.4.3_

EXEMPTIONS 1 2 3 4 5 6 7 8 9

PAGES EXEMPT _____

(2426)

air force space systems development program

(Spade 1)

70 Oct 59

AIR FORCE BALLISTIC MISSILE DIVISION, HEADQUARTERS,
AIR RESEARCH AND DEVELOPMENT COMMAND

CONFIDENTIAL

BODY-1
WDZR-180

~~CONFIDENTIAL~~ *Unclas*

AIR FORCE SPACE SYSTEMS
DEVELOPMENT PROGRAM

(2426)

Short Title: SPADE I

DOWNGRADED AT 12 YEAR
VA.S: NOT ...O. ...TICALLY
ASSIFIED, DOD D... 5200.10

20 October 1959

DOW........ER ....ERVALS;
...... R 12 YEA....
..200.10

AIR FORCE BALLISTIC MISSILE DIVISION
HEADQUARTERS
AIR RESEARCH AND DEVELOPMENT COMMAND

~~CONFIDENTIAL~~ *Unclas*

....-180

i

Cy No. 2 of 50 Cys.

 This document contains information affecting the national defense of the United States within the meaning of the Espionage Laws, Title

CONFIDENTIAL

FOREWORD

There exists an urgent need to define and initiate a coordinated Air Force Space Systems Program. The following pages outline in broad terms a space program based on established Air Force General Operational Requirements plus other requirements which appear to be necessary to complete and integrate the over-all program. This planning guide, which we call SPADE for "Space Development", has the following objectives:

1. To delineate Air Force space requirements;

2. To define the systems under development or being considered to meet these requirements; and

3. To promote the recognition and advancement of the technology needed to achieve the systems.

This initial report, which is very preliminary, is designed to serve as the framework for continuing study. It is to be modified periodically as the need arises.

This document is intended as a tool to assist in coordinating and ordering the Air Force space program definition and development, and is for the use of using commands in defining operational requirements, and centers and laboratories in analyzing development requirements. With the assistance of interested commands and agencies, the study ultimately should define and provide an analysis of each of the required systems in sufficient detail to show the inter-relationship of the various technical requirements. The results of this analysis will indicate critical areas in which technological advancements are required to permit timely development of systems to accomplish the space-age missions.

OSMOND J. RITLAND   for
Major General, USAF
Commander

CONFIDENTIAL

WDZR-180
ii

SECRET

This document contains information affecting the national defense of the United States within the meaning of the Espionage Laws, Title 18 U.S.C. Section 793 and 794

TABLE OF CONTENTS

CONFIDENTIAL

WDZR-180

 This document contains information affecting the national defense of the United States w........................rs. This

CONFIDENTIAL

TABLE OF CONTENTS

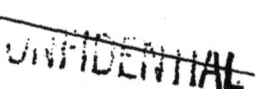

CONFIDENTIAL

CONFIDENTIAL iv

This document contains information affecting the national defense of the United States within the meaning of the Espionage Laws, Title 18, U.S.C., Section 793 and 794, the transmission or revelation of which in any manner to an unauthorized person is prohibited by law.

BODY-5

 CONFIDENTIAL

TABLE OF CONTENTS

BODY-6

This document contains information affecting the national defense of the United States within the meaning of the Espionage Laws, Title 18, U.S.C., Section 793 and 794, the transmission or revelation of which in any manner to an unauthorized person is prohibited by law.

CONFIDENTIAL

TABLE OF CONTENTS

This document contains information affecting the national defense of the United States within the meaning of the Espionage Laws, Title 18, U.S.C., Section 793 and 794, the transmission or revelation of which in any manner to an unauthorized person is prohibited by law.

BODY-7

I. Introduction

 CONFIDENTIAL

AN AIR FORCE SPACE SYSTEMS DEVELOPMENT PROGRAM

I. INTRODUCTION

The competition among nations in introducing new military weapon systems has become very critical with the development of the nuclear warhead and thereafter the long-range ballistic missile as a carrier for this warhead. Today, as the ballistic missile systems are becoming operational, our nation faces new and intense competition in the exploitation of weapons systems utilizing space vehicles and satellites. Our greatest threat is from an opposing nation which recognizes the military value of space operations, is capable of extreme control and acceleration of development effort, and will probably not, in actuality, conform to any international agreements for "peaceful use only" of space. With this in mind, our nation must lose no time in defining and initiating a coordinated military space systems program.

WDZR-180

 CONFIDENTIAL

This document contains information affecting the national defense of the United States within the meaning of the Espionage Laws, Title 18, U.S.C., Section 793 and 794, the transmission or revelation of which in any manner to an unauthorized person is prohibited by law.

CONFIDENTIAL

B. Evolution of a Weapons System

System operational requirements normally are initiated by the using command or by a senior plans and requirements Air Staff agency on the basis of an analysis of a mission and broad studies of potential systems capabilities. The relative priorities of the operational requirements are established by consideration of the national strategy or concept of operation, the state-of-the-art in the particular field, and the anticipated systems costs for development, maintenance and operation.

The operational requirements are converted to system development requirements through operational concept studies and preliminary design analysis. This effort involves an analysis and study of similar existing and planned systems and a study of the pertinent state-of-the-art. The results are normally preliminary development or design specifications.

The preliminary design specifications are converted into a system design by detailed design studies involving extensive selectivity studies and tests of major components for the system. If the system is unique in that it is a considerable extension of operational techniques and technical capabilities, a feasibility demonstration may be required preceding the design studies.

The system design is converted to a production design by further study, and production and tests of development prototypes. Subsequent to final design the system is produced and appropriate operational suitability and reliability tests are conducted. Modifications are made as necessary and the system is put into operational use.

WDZR-180

I-2

CONFIDENTIAL

This document contains information affecting the national defense of the United States within the meaning of the Espionage Laws, Title 18, U.S.C., Section 793 and 794, the transmission or revelation of which in any manner to an unauthorized person is prohibited by law.

This sequence of events for a major weapon system usually covers a period of from 5-10 years. Most weapon systems involve a major extension of the state-of-the-art for development of one or more of the major components. This is particularly true in military space systems development. If the systems currently under development and anticipated can be defined and analyzed in sufficient detail to show the inter-relationships of the various technical requirements, it should be possible to foresee some of the critical technological advancements required to permit timely development of the systems.

C. Purpose of the SPADE Plan

The purpose of the SPADE Plan is to guide space system planning by assembling and discussing space system requirements, analyzing the systems under development or being considered to meet the requirements, and correlating the major component requirements in principal areas to permit relatively economical and timely development. Timely identi-fication and promotion of the state-of-the-art improvement in critical areas is a major long-range goal of this plan.

Section II, which follows, contains a listing and descriptions of Air Force space systems requirements. These requirements, for the most part, are based on established General Operational Requirements issued by Headquarters USAF. An effort has been made to indicate a general priority for some requirements.

Systems which may fill certain of these requirements are dis-cussed in Sections III and IV. In Section III are included systems which are in operation, in development, or in the advanced planning stage. These systems have been analyzed in some detail and can be defined reasonably well. Section IV describes systems which are under study or which are being considered but are in a provisional category pending study and analysis. Characteristics and design details for the latter systems are either very tentative or unknown.

Section V lists long-range systems studies designed to investigate concepts and areas from which future systems designs may be drawn.

This document contains information affecting the national defense of the United States within the meaning of the Espionage Laws, Title 18, U.S.C., Section 793 and 794, the transmission or revelation of which in any manner to an unauthorized person is prohibited by law.

These studies play a key part in the evolution of a weapon system, for their results suggest new requirements and point the way toward systems which may some day fulfill advanced requirements.

Section VI contains descriptions of major test support systems or programs which are required or may be directly applicable to the space weapon research and development program.

Section VII contains a discussion of systems analysis and sub-system correlation. Included are a consolidated schedule of all of the space systems programs and a summary of system specifications or characteristics for these systems which have progressed to the specification stage. These charts, which are very preliminary at this time, serve to illustrate the usefulness of the SPADE Plan and the effort to be associated with the Plan. As additional space systems are analyzed and the schedule and characteristics are defined more clearly, the data in the charts will become more apparent.

Section VIII describes an analysis of Air Force Space Booster requirements. The correlation between individual system booster requirements and a proposed development program for this major subsystem area is explained. The intent to analyze other areas of major component technological development and state-of-the-art advancement is stated.

Certain conclusions are drawn in Section IX.

Appendix "A" contains selected definitions, and Appendix "B" contains a number of references applicable to the system discussed in the SPADE Plan. The complete booster analysis paper is included as Appendix "C", and a list of representative development and research areas which are or could support military space systems development is contained in Appendix "D".

This document contains information affecting the national defense of the United States within the meaning of the Espionage Laws, Title 18, U.S.C., Section 793 and 794, the transmission or revelation of which in any manner to an unauthorized person is prohibited by law.

II. Military Space Systems Requirements

II. MILITARY SPACE SYSTEMS REQUIREMENTS

The following section surveys the various military operations associated with aerospace as an operating medium. It expresses these operations as Military Space System Requirements. These requirements, together with an indication of the status of programs to satisfy them, are summarized in Table II-1 and described in some detail in the following pages. Although an attempt is made to examine the entire range of possible requirements, it is well for the reader to keep in mind the systems of clearly-recognized, early military interest, to-wit:

Strategic communications

Reconnaissance

Ballistic missiles

Missile and satellite defense

These areas are of early, definite interest, because it is now evident that powerful, even decisive, military advantages are to be gained therein. We are, of course, continuing to analyze other areas of space weapon possibilities for systems of considerable potential.

Of the currently-recognized space system requirements, both communications and reconnaissance offer clear, concrete military advantages. In each of these areas, systems can be developed now which will contribute powerfully to our national military posture.

It has not yet been possible to focus quite so clearly upon the basic area of strategic offensive-defensive forces, due to the depth of the un-plumbed technology involved. The strategic potential of the ICBM, which traverses space for 90 per cent of its trajectory, is understood very well. However, the full value of space as an operating medium within which to blunt or frustrate an enemy ICBM attack is not yet completely understood.

Potentially, though, it is possible to recognize the overwhelming military advantage accruing to the nation which first couples a useful

WDZR-180

II-1

 CONFIDENTIAL

This document contains information affecting the national defense of the United States within the meaning of the Espionage Laws, Title 18, U.S.C., Section 793 and 794, the transmission or revelation of which in any manner to an unauthorized person is prohibited by law.

TABLE II.1

SUMMARY OF MILITARY SPACE SYSTEMS

MISSION	SYSTEM REQUIREMENT	ACTIVE AND PLANNED	UNDER STUDY
A. Offensive	1. Strategic Missile (GOR 180)	THOR, ATLAS, TITAN, MINUTEMAN, ALBM	SR 199
	2. Bombardment Satellite (GOR 174)		SR 181
	3. Tactical Weapon System		
	4. Deception and Jamming		
B. Defense	1. Missile Attack Alarm (GOR 80)	MIDAS	
	2. Ballistic Missile Defense (GOR 156)		AICBM
	3. Satellite Defense (GOR 170)	SAINT	
C. Surveillance	1. Visual and/or Infrared (GOR 80)	SAMOS	SR 178
	2. Ferret (GOR 80)		
	3. Mapping (GOR 80)	SAMOS	SR 178
	4. Weapon Test Surveillance	SAMOS	SR 178 Test Surveillance (VALA)
D. Communications	1. Ground-Air Polar (GOR 178)	STEER (R and D only); SAC Polar	
	2. Ground-Ground Equatorial (GOR 178)	TACKLE/DECREE (R and D only); FLAG (National Survival)	
F. Support	1. Environmental Observing and Forecast (GOR 176)	TIROS (NASA R and D)	
	2. Space Navigation Aid	TRANSIT (Navy R and D)	
	3. Logistic Support of Space Operations		
	4. Rescue		
	5. Satellite Tracking and Cataloguing	SPACE TRACK	

WDZR-180

This document contains information affecting the national defense of the United States within the meaning of the Espionage Laws, Title 18, U.S.C., Section 793 and 794, the transmission or revelation of which in any manner to an unauthorized person is prohibited by law.

ICBM defense with its decisive offensive strength. That nation will, if it desires to use it, possess the capability to shape a stable world order.

In the more likely possibility that both the opposing nations achieve approximate defensive parity, then a tremendous need for further offensive improvements can be anticipated. Thus, in the classic military pattern, the alternative move and counter-move of developing military capabilities may be expected.

Consider, for example, the possibilities generated by the development of an orbiting defensive system which intercepts and destroys ballistic missiles during the boost or powered-flight phase. Such an achievement immediately initiates an effort to provide powerful satellite interceptor systems, to attack the defenses; orbiting bombardment systems, which can be launched innocuously from the ground; or advanced missiles which can evade or similarly frustrate the defenders during powered flight. Thus evolves the ever-changing spectrum of military requirements and defense expenditures.

The pages which follow discuss individually the military space system requirements which presently can be foreseen. Some of the requirements may appear Buck Rogerish to those not in frequent contact with space system activity. This is not the case. Many of these systems are feasible within the 1960-65 period, and others which now appear quite extreme can be available in the 1965-75 era if selected and emphasized development effort is initiated at a reasonably early date. In this connection, it should be remembered that the complexity and cost of current weapon systems have restricted the U. S. to a few selected systems. The military leaders now know the number and kind of weapons to be provided in the foreseeable future for defense of the U. S. As time progresses, costly incremental improvement of current systems could be accomplished. However, it appears to be almost mandatory that we take a quantum jump into space, and develop selected active defense as well as deterrent space weapon systems.

WDZR-180

II-3

 CONFIDENTIAL

This document contains information affecting the national defense of the United States within the meaning of the Espionage Laws, Title 18, U.S.C., Section 793 and 794, the transmission or revelation of which in any manner to an unauthorized person is prohibited by law.

 CONFIDENTIAL

A. Offense Missions

The projection of our national ICBM deterrent force capabilities into the realm of space should be accomplished by a logical transition from its current configuration into improved ICBM weapon system capabilities coupled possibly with a low altitude orbiting bombardment system. A companion satellite reconnaissance and intelligence system will also be necessary to support our national defense and counter offense efforts. Extension of our initial low altitude system to a manned satellite might be foreseen during the 1965-1975 period.

1. Strategic Missile

GOR 180 establishes the requirement for an advanced or improved ICBM weapon system whose initial range and payload will provide the means to increase our operational flexibility and expand our counter-offensive capabilities.

Technical evaluation of the current ICBM weapon systems and the state-of-the-art of missile and associated technology indicate it is possible to improve these systems to the degree where a 9,000 nautical mile, greater than 5-megaton payload capability could be realized at an early date. Study should be continued in this area, and a restatement of R and D product improvement and AEC development should be obtained and evaluated.

In discussing advanced ICBM operational systems, consideration must be given to the effectiveness of a large number of relatively low yield missiles with adequate range, great accuracy, low vulnerability, and logistic support simplicity, versus a smaller number of high yield missiles that have adequate range and yield but are inherently more expensive due to logistic and support problems. Since "time" and "cost" appear to be two of our more critical commodities, the early availability, increased reliability, and cost effectiveness of the lower yield weapons may be our best near-term objective. The long-term goal could continue to be the high yield warhead or comparable

WDZR-180

II-4

 CONFIDENTIAL

This document contains information affecting the national defense of the United States within the meaning of the Espionage Laws, Title 18, U.S.C., Section 793 and 794, the transmission or revelation of which in any manner to an unauthorized person is prohibited by law.

BODY-17

kill capability, with the objective of achieving breakthroughs in the state-of-the-art that would provide the higher yield in a light warhead with the associated accuracy, logistic simplicity, and low vulnerability.

Specific requirements for the advanced/improved ICBM missile state a range of 8,500 miles, with a payload capability for nuclear warheads in the 20-50 megaton range and CEP of one nautical mile. This capability will permit the using command to locate its launch sites anywhere in the ZI USA, and provides strike capabilities for coverage of USSR (and its Asiatic Communist-dominated countries) industrial and metropolitan target areas. A counter-offense capability against enemy ICBM launch installations located as far south as the Malayan Penninsula may also be realized. The capability represents an advance in the ground-based U.S. ICBM deterrent force, supplementing the strategic manned bomber force. However, the need to increase the deterrent threat and provide improved operational techniques, particularly in the counter defense and penetration areas, through the medium of air-launched and satellite-launched orbiting vehicles, establishes the additional requirement for development of a strategic bombardment satellite.

Air-launched and submarine-launched ballistic missiles provide certain operational advantages over both the ground-launched missile and the cruise-type stand-off weapon. In the first instance, they offer extreme launch-site dispersion, mobility, and flexibility. In the second instance, the stand-off weapon acquires the performance to overcome enemy defenses.

(Reference: THOR, Section III-A-1

ATLAS, Section III-A-2

TITAN, Section III-A-3

MINUTEMAN, Section III-A-4

ALBM, Section III-A-5

Advanced Strategic Missile, Section IV-A-1)
(See sections indicated for system descriptions)

WDZR-180

 CONFIDENTIAL

This document contains information affecting the national defense of the United States within the meaning of the Espionage Laws, Title 18, U.S.C., Section 793 and 794, the transmission or revelation of which in any manner to an unauthorized person is prohibited by law.

2. <u>Bombardment Satellite</u>

The feasibility and practicality of a bombardment satellite must be carefully studied. The most obvious concept for a bombardment satellite is a nuclear warhead in orbit about the Earth so that the plane of its orbit passes over or near all potential targets. Thus, a polar orbit would bring all areas of the world under orbit within a twelve-hour period. The warhead-carrying satellite could thus be launched at leisure in orbit around the Earth, with the capability of being triggered out of orbit when one so desires. The selection of orbits for a bombardment satellite must be carefully considered so that all potential targets come under coverage of the satellite force and that the destruction is such as to optimize the desired target concentration and minimize the vulnerability of the satellite to a satellite defense system. For use of a satellite as a bombardment vehicle, the warhead must descend essentially intact through the Earth's atmosphere to the target. Since the warhead descends on a ballistic trajectory to the target when the orbital velocity is reduced, this point of reduced velocity must be carefully predetermined in order to provide the required range accuracy. Detailed control of the velocity of ejection from orbit will be required to achieve acceptable accuracies. In addition, some control in azimuth will be required since only a rare coincidence would place an intended target in the orbital plane of the satellite. To achieve azimuth control, a component of velocity must be provided normal to the plane of the orbit.

The development of a strategic bombardment satellite is an established requirement (GOR 174). The research and development, and subsequent operational employment in space of an armed nuclear satellite, by the U.S. must consider the political and world-wide ramifications in the event of an unforeseen incident which may cause impact on friendly or enemy territory. Therefore, absolute control must exist in all satellites carrying conventional and nuclear armament, and specific sea areas must be designated for impact and recovery of

WDZR-180

 CONFIDENTIAL II-6

This document contains information affecting the national defense of the United States within the meaning of the Espionage Laws, Title 18, U.S.C., Section 793 and 794, the transmission or revelation of which in any manner to an unauthorized person is prohibited by law.

erratic and malfunctioning satellites. Positive means of cataloguing and identifying U.S. satellites must also exist for control of this system.

General development parameters for the strategic bombardment satellite are as follows: The mission will be to supplement the national strategic deterrent force. It must have the characteristics for providing continuous alert, low vulnerability, long life (reliability) and low cost. Control and cataloguing functions should be within the capabilities of current or proposed military systems, and/or modifications or additions to existing equipment. System and subsystem developments should permit injection and ejection of multiple counter defense and penetration aid devices. Outside skin should be non-reflective radar absorbent type. Simplicity, protection against neutralization, and positive warhead arming and disarming control features are other development objectives. (Reference: Bombardment Satellite, Section IV-A-2.)

3. Tactical Weapon System

A vigorous study of the application of large ballistic missiles to tactical military operation is required to establish the feasibility and potential availability of systems capable of performing missions of the tactical air command, when it is no longer feasible to use conventional aircraft. Operational objectives such as the attack of mobile military targets, battlefield reconnaissance, and the delivery of massive destruction against concentrated field forces, should be evaluated for solution by the use of ballistic missiles or space vehicles. The need for this type of weapon, or the utility of ballistic missiles for this application, will be determined by further study. (Reference: Tactical Weapon System, Section IV-A-3.)

4. Deception and Jamming

In studies which have been conducted to define satellite defense systems, consideration was given to the possibility that the

WDZR-180

II-7

 CONFIDENTIAL

This document contains information affecting the national defense of the United States within the meaning of the Espionage Laws, Title 18, U.S.C., Section 793 and 794, the transmission or revelation of which in any manner to an unauthorized person is prohibited by law.

enemy might use decoys and jamming. Therefore, it appears that there is a requirement for a system capable of this type of action for use with U.S. satellites. In addition, consideration should be given to the possibility of jamming enemy communications from a satellite as an offensive measure. (Reference: Deception and Jamming, Section IV-A-4.)

B. Defense Missions

It is axiomatic that enemy capability to deliver decisive military force against us through any operating medium requires our immediate attention toward means of denying him this advantage. Space is such an operating medium, and the ballistic missile has become an instrument of decisive military force. Development of a missile defense system thus becomes our initial space defensive concern. Our ability to effectively employ such a defense will, in turn, call upon counter-ingenuity by the enemy, leading through more versatile missiles to offensive satellite schemes, with an eventual probability of manned offensive systems. Our defensive development timetable must keep up with the enemy pace and should, of course, be designed to get out in front. By overtaking the enemy here, so as to couple our offensive might with an effective defense, the U.S. can again establish a favorable balance of international power, making possible the achievement of a stable peace. The discussions that follow concern these defensive requirements.

1. Missile Attack Alarm

A requirement for a system capable of surveillance for early warning of ballistic missile attack was established by GOR 80.

The infrared reconnaissance subsystem (Alert System), which is to provide instantaneous alarm of attack by ICBM's, is required on a most urgent basis with an initial capability at the very earliest date. The operational objective is to detect the launching of ICBM's, immediately alert the active missile defense system to such launchings, then track the ICBM's to positively determine that the attack is aimed

WDZR-180

II-8

This document contains information affecting the national defense of the United States within the meaning of the Espionage Laws, Title 18, U.S.C., Section 793 and 794, the transmission or revelation of which in any manner to an unauthorized person is prohibited by law.

 CONFIDENTIAL

at the U. S. or its possessions. Long-range plans envision the incorporation of the infrared detection and tracking capability into a manned space defense vehicle system. (Reference: MIDAS, Section III-B-1, and Advanced Attack Alarm, Section IV-B-1.)

2. Ballistic Missile Defense

The Soviet Union has, or will have shortly, an ICBM capability that is a threat to our nation. Satellites launched by the Russians indicate they have rocket engines and guidance systems which are sufficiently developed to allow them to direct an ICBM attack against the U. S. There is some question as to the actual number of Russian ICBM's that can be launched immediately; however, they must be assumed to have a production capability at least equal to our own. During 1960 the Russians may be expected to achieve the capability of launching a decisive ICBM attack.

A requirement for a ballistic missile defense system was established by GOR 156.

The objective of a ballistic missile or an anti-missile defense system is to prevent the detonation of the nose cone warhead in the intended target area. The three phases of an ICBM trajectory (acceleration, coasting, and deceleration) define three general classes of anti-missile defense schemes. These are commonly referred to as the "during boost", "mid-course", and "re-entry" approaches.

Regardless of the approach selected, an anti-missile system must provide for the detection and tracking of the nose cone vehicle until it can be diverted or destroyed by interceptor weapons. The maximum flight time is of the order of thirty-five minutes so that an effective defensive system must have a very quick reaction time.

Analysis of the three types of anti-missiles indicates that the ICBM is most vulnerable during the boost phase of its trajectory when detection and tracking of the nose cone vehicle are relatively simple since the attached booster is optically visible for hundreds of

 CONFIDENTIAL

WDZR-180

This document contains information affecting the national defense of the United States within the meaning of the Espionage Laws, Title 18, U.S.C., Section 793 and 794, the transmission or revelation of which in any manner to an unauthorized person is prohibited by law.

miles. During this period infrared seeker missiles with non-nuclear warheads could divert the warhead by destroying booster guidance and/or thrust. This approach cannot be pursued initially due to our present inability to operate from satellite bases with the required degree of reliability and economy of effort.

It appears that early anti-missile systems, if mandatory, will have to be developed around ground-based interceptors which destroy the warhead during the mid-course or re-entry portions of its trajectory. Considerable study will be required before adoption of a ground-based system. Powerful radar equipment will be required to illuminate the ICBM-warhead for detection and tracking. Methods must be found to discriminate between this warhead and the swarms of decoys which are expected. Large interceptor missiles equipped with nuclear warheads will probably be required to insure destruction of the very rugged ICBM warhead. This, in turn, will place severe altitude restrictions on the interceptor to prevent thermal or blast damage to friendly territory. Such restrictions make the mid-course attack more attractive than the re-entry approach.

Another prime requirement of an anti-missile defense system is a warning element to alert our strategic offensive forces as well as the civil and military defense agencies. For maximum warning, surveillance satellites over enemy launch sites are required. Passive IR sensors will be used to detect ICBM boosters as they rise above the atmosphere. Interim warning systems, however, will use ground-based radar or airborne IR equipment deployed as closely as possible to the potential missile launching areas.

3. Satellite Defense

The objective of a satellite defense system is to catalogue and inspect unidentified satellites and to disable those orbiting satellites found undesirable by the U.S. The system should have peacetime as well as wartime potentialities. This indicates a kill mechanism which is more surreptitious (and less disruptive to radio communications, etc.)

WDZR-180

II-10

 CONFIDENTIAL

This document contains information affecting the national defense of the United States within the meaning of the Espionage Laws, Title 18, U.S.C., Section 793 and 794, the transmission or revelation of which in any manner to an unauthorized person is prohibited by law.

BODY-23

than nuclear destruction of the satellite. GOR 170 establishes the requirement for a satellite defense system.

The ability to catalogue and disable enemy satellites becomes urgently required at such time as Russia could, through satellites, significantly threaten our national security. Present Russian satellites threaten only our prestige and complacency. Near-immediate Russian capabilities include using satellites for reconnaissance, surveillance, and counter-measures (electronic and saturation) against our ICBM early-warning and defensive systems. This latter Russian capability indicates an urgent requirement for a cataloguing capability. By 1963-1965, satellites might be used to track (infrared) our missiles so as to actively facilitate the Russian ICBM defense system. We should counter these with an active ability to disable enemy satellites. This ability would also be applicable against Soviet bombardment satellites, which might exist by 1965 if our missile defenses made the Russians employ such weapons, and against Russian satellite-launched anti-ICBM missiles possible by 1965-1970.

The anti-satellite system will include elements which locate, identify, inspect, and neutralize enemy satellites. Initial interceptors will probably be unmanned ground-launched systems, with follow-on manned identification and neutralizing forces stationed in orbit, as the art permits. Threatening satellites may be in orbits varying from 100 to several thousand miles. Sizes may vary from 5 to 50 feet, and weights from 100 to 25,000 pounds. Large numbers of decoys, combined with numerous "spoofing" opportunities, will make target identification and discrimination one of the severest problems facing an effective, practicable system. For good political and technical reasons, killing with nuclear weapons may be unwise. Careful inspection and kill assessment require the proximity feature of a rendezvous type vehicle as an alternative to nuclear destruction of the hostile satellite. Initial defensive force requirements will tend to be reduced by systems permitting several orbital passes by the

WDZR-180

II-11

CONFIDENTIAL

This document contains information affecting the national defense of the United States within the meaning of the Espionage Laws, Title 18, U.S.C., Section 793 and 794, the transmission or revelation of which in any manner to an unauthorized person is prohibited by law.

BODY-24

hostile satellite. Ground control systems must include or tie in with "space track" or similar satellite acquisition, tracking and cataloguing systems.

The problem of distinguishing satellite threats from decoys arises, of course, when the threats materialize. As indicated above, 1963-1965 could bring a grave threat in the form of satellite components of an effective Russian ICBM defense. The initial U. S. satellite defense system must cope with this problem. By 1965-1970, the increasing Russian capability (with recoverable booster) to economically infest space with scientific probes, multi-ton satellites, jammers, debris, bombs, ICBM detectors and interceptors, and multitudes of decoys will require an advanced interceptor/inspection system to cope with the problem. (Reference: SAINT, Section III-B-2.)

C. Surveillance Missions

Advanced surveillance systems are required to provide aerial world-wide reconnaissance, to provide strategic intelligence data, and to support international inspection systems. The systems devised will be companions to the advanced offensive and defensive space systems being considered and consequently must be compatible with these systems.

GOR 80 establishes a requirement for Reconnaissance Satellite Weapon Systems to provide the necessary reconnaissance capability. The satellites will be launched from stations within the U. S. into Earth orbits and will be monitored initially from ground stations in the Western Hemisphere. They will be employed in numbers required to acquire or confirm data concerning actions, locations, capabilities, and vulnerability of manned and unmanned strike forces. Separate or combined configurations of the photographic, electronic, infrared or other sensors will be employed to provide the desired coverage. Each satellite will require the capability of in-flight processing of data collected and transmission to ground stations or to other satellites

WDZR-180

II-12

CONFIDENTIAL

This document contains information affecting the national defense of the United States within the meaning of the Espionage Laws, Title 18, U.S.C., Section 793 and 794, the transmission or revelation of which in any manner to an unauthorized person is prohibited by law.

electronically and/or by physical transfer techniques (including re-entry and recovery). Man will undoubtedly have a place in this system, ultimately, to provide on-the-spot decisions and equipment control and repair.

The Reconnaissance Satellite subsystems are:

1. Visual and/or IR Satellite

The Visual and/or IR Reconnaissance Subsystem is to provide source material for the production of intelligence information, target materials, air navigation and topographic maps, and weather data primarily in the form of cloud cover. This operation involves aerial photography, on-board processing of film, and return of data to ground stations. Development will involve progression from lesser to greater resolution as the state-of-the-art in satellite reconnaissance improves. Initial general coverage with 100 foot resolution and spot coverage with 20-foot resolution with twelve months life will provide some capability. In future systems, general coverage with 10-foot resolution and spot coverage with 1-foot resolution with a three to five year life is desired. (References: SAMOS, Section III-C-1, and High Resolution System, Section IV-C-1.)

2. Ferret

The Electronic Reconnaissance (Ferret) Subsystem is to intercept electromagnetic emissions from potential enemies, to store the information until a time suitable for retransmission, then to transfer the intercepted information in a secure maneuver to a central intelligence station. Intercept coverage in the band of frequencies between 30 MCS and 40 KMC's is required. A direction finding capability to an accuracy of five miles is desired but its incorporation should not delay the availability of the initial version of the Ferret subsystem. It may be desirable to incorporate the Ferret subsystem with the Visual Reconnaissance subsystem. (Reference: SAMOS, Section III-C-1.)

WDZR-180

This document contains information affecting the national defense of the United States within the meaning of the Espionage Laws, Title 18, U.S.C., Section 793 and 794, the transmission or revelation of which in any manner to an unauthorized person is prohibited by law.

BODY-26

3. Mapping

The Mapping and Charting Subsystem is to provide carto-graphic agencies with photographic and radar mapping service of the land mass areas of the world, including those areas which are not presently accessible whether for political or other reasons. The end product of this subsystem must result in maps and charts (or substitutes) of geodetic accuracy. Photography produced by this subsystem must be of high quality with sufficient data recorded on the negative to facilitate reduction to usable form by cartographic agencies. High-resolution radar should provide data not available by photographic means. The required quality of the data and the quantity of information involved would appear to govern the necessity of a means of recovering the film itself in this subsystem. (Reference: SAMOS, Section III-C-1.)

4. Weapon Test Surveillance

Possible international agreements on disarmament create a need for surveillance of space to detect nuclear explosions. Even in the absence of such agreements there is an intelligence requirement for such data. (Reference: Weapons Test Surveillance, Section IV-C-2.)

D. Communications Mission

The communications satellite provides a relay station for long-distance radio communications. Initial applications are ground/ground and ground/air; later applications will require links between the various elements of complex military space forces. GOR 178 describes the requirement for a communications relay satellite system for ground/ground and ground/air communication.

Satellite communications relay for military operations control promises relative invulnerability from certain critical enemy threats against other communications means. A particularly pressing need, that for over-the-pole communication with SAC bomber forces, can be achieved using 5,600-mile polar satellites. An extremely hard

This document contains information affecting the national defense of the United States within the meaning of the Espionage Laws, Title 18, U.S.C., Section 793 and 794, the transmission or revelation of which in any manner to an unauthorized person is prohibited by law.

world-wide (exclusive of polar regions) system can be achieved using 22,700-nautical mile "synchronous" satellites. The first space-to-space communications applications could well accompany missile-warning (and later, missile-tracking) satellite systems. Each major weapon system advance after that will require increased space communication capabilities.

Initial communications satellites must include sensitive, jam-resistant receivers and transmitters as well as precision attitude control for antenna positioning. Urgent developments include long-life power sources, such as big arrays of solar cells, and large payloads to permit high volumes of data transmission. Military space communications will have to devote great emphasis to light, long-lived, reliable and secure systems. The communications advantages of space long line-of-sight ranges and freedom of atmospheric and ionospheric attenuation between suitably positioned space vehicles, must be fully exploited. As payloads and secondary power sources permit, satellite-borne jamming equipment will offer advantages in space-era ECM.

(Reference: STEER, Section III-D-1

TACKLE/DECREE, Section III-D-2

SAC Polar Satellite, Section III-D-3

FLAG, Section III-D-4

COURIER, Section III-D-5

Global Communication Satellite, Section IV-D-1)

E. Supporting Missions

There are numerous categories of space activity which we must master to acquire the primary mission capabilities discussed before. Some of these "supporting" space missions will be initially employed in support of non-space operations. In general, though, these early

WDZR-180

This document contains information affecting the national defense of the United States within the meaning of the Espionage Laws, Title 18, U.S.C., Section 793 and 794, the transmission or revelation of which in any manner to an unauthorized person is prohibited by law.

BODY-28

accomplishments will provide the know-how required later for vital support of operational space systems. The following paragraphs discuss several of these supporting systems which will ultimately provide important elements of the technology permitting military operations in space.

1. Environmental Observing and Forecasting

As military operations are extended beyond the Earth's atmosphere the need will grow for an integrated system to coordinate the observing and forecasting of environmental conditions which the space missions will encounter. GOR 176 establishes a requirement for such a system to extend and supplement the present weather observing and forecasting system.

The primary function of the system is that of furnishing environment reporting and forecasting support to space vehicles operating above 200,000 feet. A secondary function is observation of weather in support of a Weather Observing and Forecasting System. This system would operate much the same as the existing weather system insofar as processing and analyzing the environmental data and distributing forecasts and information to interested commands.

The environmental data would be procured from special meteorological satellites or from multi-purpose satellites and other space craft. Development of space environment observation and reporting procedures and equipment must be coordinated with the development of other space systems, in particular the reconnaissance satellites, in order that the environmental observations may be procured from such satellites and from other space craft as an associated function of such vehicle operations where practicable. Development of this system should parallel the development of the family of space weapons to provide the timely incorporation of environmental reporting components and procedures into the design of each system where feasible. (Reference: TIROS, Section III-E-1.)

 CONFIDENTIAL
II-16

This document contains information affecting the national defense of the United States within the meaning of the Espionage Laws, Title 18, U.S.C., Section 793 and 794, the transmission or revelation of which in any manner to an unauthorized person is prohibited by law.

2. Space Navigation Aid

Navigation aids placed in orbit promise certain aids to
position determination on or near the Earth's surface. Ultimately,
"beacons" in terrestrial and cislunar space will facilitate the positioning
or navigating of military satellites and space vehicles. This requirement is not specifically called out in an established GOR, since the
need can be expected to arise primarily as an outgrowth of specific
mission-system requirements.

The basic time requisite is to acquire sufficient experience,
through early experimental efforts, in order to meet requirements
which will be defined as future military space systems, and should
receive careful design consideration. Defensive systems involving
large numbers of patrolling satellites might well utilize positional
reference satellites to maintain necessary control of far-flung forces.
Later operations involving maneuverable defensive patrols, possibly
extending to cislunar ranges, may call on further navigational assistance,
perhaps from "fixed" 24-hour or libration-point satellites.

Various doppler and hyperbolic schemes may find applications. Objectives will be to supplement stellar references with
favorably located "beacons" nearer the operational arena. It is most
likely that navigation schemes will depend upon requirements of the
missions of the over-all weapon systems. (Reference: TRANSIT,
Section III-E-3, and Advanced Navigation, Section IV-E-1.)

3. Logistic Support of Space Operations (recoverable boosters, maintenance and re-supply, space transportation)

The deployment and use of integrated offensive and
defensive space systems, ultimately requiring scores and possibly
hundreds of cooperating, functioning satellites, will pose challenging
logistic problems. To operate effectively in space, we must solve
these problems. We must economically get these large numbers of
satellites into orbit and then replace (or augment) them as they wear

This document contains information affecting the national defense of the United States within the meaning of the Espionage Laws, Title 18, U.S.C., Section 793 and 794, the transmission or revelation of which in any manner to an unauthorized person is prohibited by law.

BODY-30

out. Ultimately, we must be able to repair or re-supply the basic satellite vehicles. Finally, when man begins functioning in space, we will have problems in personnel transportation. Existing GOR's (80, 170, 174) which may be met by orbital systems involving large numbers of satellites establish the urgency of space logistic considerations.

Large scale systems first become feasible and required with the ICBM tracking and detection component of the missile defense system. Later, orbital anti-satellite patrols and offensive systems will be in operation. Still later, manned satellite inspection systems and other manned systems will require full-scale logistic support.

Recoverable boosters offer great economies in the deployment and replenishment of many satellite military systems. These vehicles must be available eventually in the million-pound and greater thrust class; they must be maneuverable enough (and manned, if necessary) to assure recovery essentially intact for re-use.

With more complex systems aloft, economies may eventually become feasible if malfunctioning satellites are repaired instead of replaced. Re-fueling of powered satellites which must periodically reposition themselves or must indulge in maneuvers is another such application. Requirements for rendezvous are similar to those raised by the satellite inspection (defensive systems) requirements.

Man can obviously participate very profitably in these logistic functions, and it may be here (in a non-combat environment) that he first fulfills a military role in space. If so, this will bring on requirements for personnel transportation into and out of space, and for considerations of manned space station assembly and operation. (Reference: Re-supply, Section IV-E-2, and Transport Logistics, Section IV-E-4.)

4. Rescue

A requirement exists for a satellite system capable of locating persons in distress on the Earth's surface. Reception of

 CONFIDENTIAL

This document contains information affecting the national defense of the United States within the meaning of the Espionage Laws, Title 18, U.S.C., Section 793 and 794, the transmission or revelation of which in any manner to an unauthorized person is prohibited by law.

distress signals and re-transmission with location data to a ground station can be envisioned as an early system capability. (Reference: Rescue, Section IV-E-3.)

5. Satellite Tracking and Cataloguing

The objective of the satellite tracking and cataloguing system is to detect, track, and compute orbital data for all satellites, both cooperating and non-cooperating. Specifically, a requirement for this system exists in support of the satellite defense mission. In addition, data provided by this system would be useful for intelligence purposes.

An operational space track system should have a capability of detecting dark (non-radiating) satellites passing over the continental U.S. at altitudes to 1,000 nautical miles. An increase of altitude detection capability to as much as 25,000 nautical miles is a desirable objective. The system should be capable of tracking uncooperative satellites with accuracy sufficient to provide orbital information needed by a satellite inspection system.

In addition to acquisition and tracking radars and other radio detection devices, the system must have adequate communications facilities for data transmission to a control center. The control center facilities would include computation, maintenance of a space situation display (showing locations of all satellites), and provision for threat alarm.

Detection equipment for dark satellites at altitudes to 1,000 nautical miles could be available in the 1961-1962 period. Considerable improvement in the state-of-the-art will be necessary for a significant increase of this altitude capability. (Reference: Space Track System, Section III-E-4.)

This document contains information affecting the national defense of the United States within the meaning of the Espionage Laws, Title 18, U.S.C., Section 793 and 794, the transmission or revelation of which in any manner to an unauthorized person is prohibited by law.

III. Systems: Active and Planned

SECRET CONFIDENTIAL

III. SYSTEMS: ACTIVE AND PLANNED

In this section are described systems which are in operation, in development, or planned.

A. Offense Systems

1. THOR

THOR (SM-75) is a single-stage liquid-fueled IRBM, mounted in soft surface launch complexes, which is now completing its development period.

It can be launched within fifteen minutes of fire order. Initial THOR squadrons are now operational under the RAF in Great Britain.

Mission	Strategic bombardment
Length	64 feet 10 inches
Diameter	8 feet
Weight	110, 000 pounds
Propulsion	Single engine, 150, 000 pounds thrust
Guidance	Inertial, 2 n. mi. CEP
Re-entry vehicle	Copper heat-sink
Warhead	1600 pounds
Operational range	300 to 1500 n. mi.

2. ATLAS

ATLAS (SM-65) is a stage-and-a-half liquid-fueled ICBM now approaching operational status. It can be launched within fifteen minutes of fire order. Initial squadrons will be mounted in soft surface launch complexes; later squadrons will be hard-based in underground silos. The ATLAS will be stationed within the continental United States.

Mission	Strategic bombardment
Length	82 feet 6 inches
Diameter	10 feet
Weight	266, 100 pounds
Propulsion	Booster engine: two chambers, total 300, 000 pounds thrust
	Sustainer: one 60, 000 pound chamber
Guidance	Radio guidance, 2 n. mi. CEP (inertial guidance later)
Re-entry vehicle	Copper heat-sink (ablative later)

WDZR-180

CONFIDENTIAL

This document contains information affecting the national defense of the United States within the meaning of the Espionage Laws, Title 18, U.S.C., Section 793 and 794, the transmission or revelation of which in any manner to an unauthorized person is prohibited by law.

Warhead	1600 pounds
Operational Range	2000 to 5500 n. mi. (7000 later)

3. TITAN

TITAN (SM-68) is a two-stage liquid-fueled ICBM now under-going flight tests. It will be launched within fifteen minutes of fire order. Squadrons will be deployed in underground silos capable of withstanding 100 psi overpressure. Operational capability is scheduled for mid-1961.

Mission	Strategic bombardment
Length	97 feet
Diameter	10 feet
Weight	221, 000 pounds
Propulsion	First stage: two chambers, total 300, 000 pounds thrust. Second stage: one chamber, 80, 000 pounds altitude thrust
Guidance	Radio (inertial later)
Re-entry vehicle	Ablative, 4100 pounds
Operational range	Over 5500 n. mi.

4. MINUTEMAN

MINUTEMAN (SM-80) is a three-stage solid-fueled ICBM now under development. It will be substantially smaller than ATLAS or TITAN. It can be launched in seconds after receiving fire order. Squadrons will be dispersed principally in hard underground installations, with about 25 percent of the force scheduled for mobile (railroad) deployment to further confound enemy counter-action. Operational capability is scheduled for early 1963.

Mission	Quick-reaction strategic bombardment
Length	56 feet
Diameter	5-1/2 feet
Weight	65, 400 pounds
Propulsion	First stage: 166, 000 pounds thrust. Second stage: 47, 000 pounds thrust. Third stage: 15, 500 pounds thrust
Guidance	Inertial (1 n. mi. CEP)
Re-entry Vehicle	Ablative 550 to 790 pounds
Maximum Range	5500 to 6500 miles

 CONFIDENTIAL

This document contains information affecting the national defense of the United States within the meaning of the Espionage Laws, Title 18, U.S.C., Section 793 and 794, the transmission or revelation of which in any manner to an unauthorized person is prohibited by law.

5. ALBM

WS 138 A is now under development. It will provide an air-launched ballistic missile for use in strategic bombardment.

Mission	Strategic bombardment
Length	About 50 feet
Weight	About 50,000 pounds
Propulsion	Two-stage solid propellant
Range	Approximately 1000 miles

B. Defense Systems

1. MIDAS

MIDAS is a planned satellite system which will provide, via infra-red detection of the missiles' boost flight, instantaneous early-warning of hostile ICBM attack. This technique supplements BMEWS with a different technology for greater assurance of success, as well as extending the available warning margin to approximately 25 minutes. It will become operational in 1961.

Mission	Missile attack alarm
Payload	Infra-red missile detection and instantaneous signalling
Booster	Atlas-Agena
Satellite Weight	2500 pounds
Orbit	2000 n. mi., circular, near-polar

2. SAINT

SAINT is a planned program, now being considered by Headquarters USAF, for the development of a satellite defense system. The operational system, WHITE SAINT, would be an unmanned, ground-launched system to intercept, inspect, and optionally negate satellites passing over the United States at up to 1000 miles orbital altitude. It would be operational by early 1964. GREEN SAINT would be an earlier (1962-1964) feasibility demonstration of the ground-launched co-orbital interception technique. SILVER SAINT is an investigation of a light-weight, air-launched co-planar

This document contains information affecting the national defense of the United States within the meaning of the Espionage Laws, Title 18, U.S.C., Section 793 and 794, the transmission or revelation of which in any manner to an unauthorized person is prohibited by law.

interceptor while BLUE SAINT is a study of a later manned satellite interceptor and inspector. The following table refers to the initial operational system, WHITE SAINT:

Mission	Intercept, inspect, and optionally negate unwanted satellites
Payload	Detection, communications, maneuvering and negating capabilities
Booster	Atlas-Centaur (Thor-Hydra for GREEN SAINT)
Satellite Weight	3500 pounds (1400 pounds GREEN SAINT)
Orbit	100-1000 miles, maneuverable (300 mile - GREEN SAINT)

C. Surveillance System

1. SAMOS

SAMOS is a satellite system, now approaching the flight test phase, which will provide operational military reconnaissance of the Soviet land mass. Types of coverage will include photographic, both for intelligence and for mapping, and electromagnetic ferret. The system will be operational in 1961.

Mission	Military reconnaissance
Payload	Sensing, storage, and command readout (alternative recoverable system)
Booster	Atlas-Agena
Satellite Weight	2800 pounds
Orbit	260 n.mi., near-polar circular

D. Communication Systems

1. STEER

STEER is an R and D program intended to demonstrate the feasibility of a polar satellite active communications relay for ground-to-air use. The development system will not include the orbit-keeping subsystem required for a sustained, operational system. The flight test program is scheduled for 1960-1961.

WDZR-180

III-4

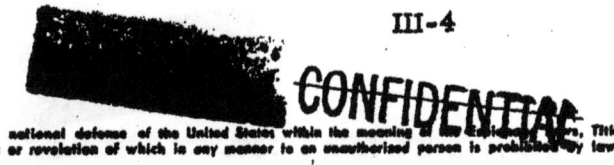 CONFIDENTIAL

This document contains information affecting the national defense of the United States within the meaning of the Espionage Laws, Title 18, U.S.C., Section 793 and 794, the transmission or revelation of which in any manner to an unauthorized person is prohibited by law.

CONFIDENTIAL

Mission	R and D for SAC Polar ground-air communications
Payload	Active, instantaneous communications repeater (WADC system)
Booster	Atlas-Agena (as in SAMOS)
Satellite Weight	400 pounds
Orbital Altitude	5600 n. mi.

2. SAC POLAR

The SAC POLAR satellite is a planned operational follow-on to STEER designed to provide secure combat-useful communications relay from ground control points to airborne SAC units in the polar regions. As such, it will provide one means of circumventing enemy and natural obstructions in maintaining positive control of the bomber fleet. The system will include eight satellites in polar orbits, with the necessary station-keeping capability to correct and maintain the orbital position. Operational date is early 1963.

Mission	SAC polar ground-air communications
Payload	Active, instantaneous communications repeater (WADC system)
Booster	Atlas-Agena (as in SAMOS)
Satellite Weight	400 pounds (minimum)
Orbital	5600 n. mi., polar

3. TACKLE/DECREE

TACKLE and DECREE are Army-managed development programs intended to demonstrate the boost, injection, and control of a communications payload in a synchronous 24-hour orbit, and to integrate the payload and satellite with the launch system. Neither program is designed to satisfy Air Force operational needs; the Army Signal Corps is the communications agency involved. TACKLE will employ ATLAS-AGENA vehicles, launched from Vandenberg AFB starting 1961, with preliminary and test versions of the DECREE payload. DECREE will use the NASA ATLAS-CENTAUR vehicle, launched from AFMTC starting in 1962.

CONFIDENTIAL

This document contains information affecting the national defense of the United States within the meaning of the Espionage Laws, Title 18, U.S.C., Section 793 and 794, the transmission or revelation of which in any manner to an unauthorized person is prohibited by law.

BODY-38

Mission	Develop synchronous communications satellite
Payload	Active, instantaneous repeater (Army Signal Corps system)
Booster	Atlas-Agena (TACKLE)-Atlas-Centaur (DECREE)
Satellite Weight	400 pounds (TACKLE) 1300 pounds (DECREE)
Orbit	5600-10,000 mile elliptical polar (TACKLE) 22,400 mile equatorial (DECREE)

4. National Survival Communications System (FLAG)

FLAG is a planned operational system, now under consideration by Hq USAF, designed to provide secure combat-useful communications relay between ground control points. It is primarily to ensure the control of our SAC retaliatory forces under conditions of enemy attack, sabotage, or nuclear blackout. The system will employ three large satellites in synchronous orbits providing redundant coverage of the North American continent and adequate coverage of the non-polar free world. The ground system will employ fixed (non-tracking) hard antennas. Operational date is late 1963.

Mission	SAC non-polar ground-ground hard facility communications
Payload	Multi-channel, jam-resistant active, instantaneous communications repeater (WADC system)
Booster	Large (SATURN class)
Satellite Weight	3-4000 pounds
Orbit	22,400 n. mi. equatorial (dog-leg injection)

5. COURIER

COURIER is an Army system providing an active, delayed communications repeater for certain of their military needs. The Air Force is scheduled to provide booster support in 1960 and 1961.

This document contains information affecting the national defense of the United States within the meaning of the Espionage Laws, Title 18, U.S.C., Section 793 and 794, the transmission or revelation of which in any manner to an unauthorized person is prohibited by law.

Mission	Army communications
Payload	Active, delayed and direct repeater
Boosters	Thor-Able Star (1960) and Atlas-Agena (1961)
Satellite Weight	500 pounds
Orbit	Circular, 500 and 1200 n. mi.

E. Support

1. TIROS

TIROS is a NASA "one-of-a-kind" experimental satellite for meteorological data gathering. The Army Signal Corps is providing the satellite while the Air Force will provide and launch the booster.

Mission	NASA meteorological experiment
Payload	Army Signal Corps
Booster	Thor-Able
Satellite Weight	270 pounds
Orbit	380 n. mi. circular

2. TRANSIT

TRANSIT is a Navy experimental system for navigational support of the Polaris submarines. The Air Force will provide the required booster.

Mission	Navy navigation
Payload	Doppler system
Boosters	THOR-ABLE STAR
Satellite Weight	215-270 pounds
Orbit	400 n. mi. circular

3. SPACE TRACK System

An interim National Space Surveillance Control Center has been established and is now operating at L. G. Hanscomb Field at Bedford, Massachusetts, under Project SPACE TRACK, Cambridge Research Center. The interim system receives tracking and observation data from various sources, and maintains a catalog of the space population. By mid-1960, the capacity of the system could be 50 objects. Specifications for the accuracy of prediction under present plans are as follows: period - 0.5 seconds; inclinations-0.1 degrees; time of ascending node - 1.0 second. at epoch.

WDZR-180

 CONFIDENTIAL

This document contains information affecting the national defense of the United States within the meaning of the Espionage Laws, Title 18, U.S.C., Section 793 and 794, the transmission or revelation of which in any manner to an unauthorized person is prohibited by law.

Inputs to the system will be from radars such as that at Trinidad, Millstone, and Canadian Millstone. The ARPA east-west fence should be providing useful data by early 1960. Ultimately, a combination of one or more fences, together with appropriately located tracking radars, will be required.

Output information will be provided to military operational commands such as NORAD and SAC, for use in assessing the threat of attack. In addition, it will be furnished directly to the SAINT satellite intercept/inspection system and other operational systems. The data will also be transmitted to intelligence agencies.

Finally, there is considerable scientific value in the data collected for universities, industry, and government laboratories.

 CONFIDENTIAL

This document contains information affecting the national defense of the United States within the meaning of the Espionage Laws, Title 18, U.S.C., Section 793 and 794, the transmission or revelation of which in any manner to an unauthorized person is prohibited by law.

IV. Systems Under Study and Provisional Systems

IV. SYSTEMS UNDER STUDY AND PROVISIONAL SYSTEMS

This section discusses systems which have not been established as feasible but which are under study or may be considered for future study toward fulfilling a system requirement.

A. Offensive System

1. Advanced Strategic Missile

Studies for advanced strategic weapon systems are now underway. There are several directions in which advancing technology may turn out to promise real operational advantages over MINUTEMAN and its contemporaries. It appears that study-type effort will suffice for several years. Areas under technological and operational investigation include:

(i) Increases in gross payload, perhaps to 100,000 pounds

(ii) Provision of highway mobility

(iii) Improvement of accuracy

(iv) Hardening of ground and flight systems

(v) Command control after launch for recall or attack changes

2. Bombardment Satellite

Various current studies indicate the technological feasibility of a bombardment satellite. The question of its ultimate operational usefulness remains to be established, and merits continuing attention. This is particularly advisable in light of the disadvantages of prior Soviet recognition of the direct or psychological utility of this weapon.

3. Tactical Weapon Systems

An Air Force study is desirable in this area.

 CONFIDENTIAL

This document contains information affecting the national defense of the United States within the meaning of the Espionage Laws, Title 18, U.S.C., Section 793 and 794, the transmission or revelation of which in any manner to an unauthorized person is prohibited by law.

4. <u>Deception and Jamming</u>

Physical deception, simulation, and jamming are properly
considered as adjuncts to almost any military space system under study.
However, the area of specific systems intended primarily to frustrate
enemy tracking, defensive or communications systems merits separate
study starting right now.

B. <u>Defensive Systems</u>

1. <u>Advanced Attack Alarm</u>

The MIDAS program includes studies of possible follow-on
infra-red systems incorporating missile tracking and trajectory prediction.

2. <u>Ballistic Missile Defense</u>

Preliminary studies have been made of various ways to
defend against attacks from intercontinental ballistic missiles. The
defense of localized critical target areas is presently under development
in the NIKE ZEUS program sponsored by the Army. The main deficiencies
of this system appear to be its very high cost for defending a very limited
number of targets, and its inability to selectively attack incoming warheads
when accompanied by a large number of easily provided decoys. Although
intensive efforts are underway to improve the target discrimination capabilities of warning and tracking equipment, this discrimination function is
thought to be limited to the period when the re-entry bodies are within the
Earth's atmosphere. Air Force studies have concentrated on an area type
of defense which involves attacking the ballistic missile during the period
when it is being propelled into its ballistic trajectory or during the mid-
course of this flight when it is out of the Earth's atmosphere. In the
first case, the use of decoys is not believed to be feasible, and in the
second case, there is some indication that the mid-course environment
and time available might be utilized to provide a discrimination between
warheads and decoys.

WDZR-180

IV-2

CONFIDENTIAL

This document contains information affecting the national defense of the United States within the meaning of the Espionage Laws, Title 18, U.S.C., Section 793 and 794, the transmission or revelation of which in any manner to an unauthorized person is prohibited by law.

BODY-44

A number of surveillance satellites are under consideration for a system to attack ballistic missiles during the boost period. An infrared detection system similar to MIDAS would be used to detect the launching of a ballistic missile. Satellite-borne interceptor rockets would be launched to destroy the ballistic missile before its propulsion period was completed. An operational concept and rough sizing of satellite and interceptor vehicles has been made for this weapon system, but many technical problems require extensive research and development and actual space experiments before the true feasibility of this program can be definitely established.

The alternate system for destroying an intercontinental ballistic missile attack is to attack the ICBM's during the mid-course of the ballistic trajectory. This system is entirely dependent upon the availability of equipment capable of discriminating between war-heads and decoys traveling at very high velocities in a spherical volume of approximately 100 miles in diameter. Although the maximum range of 50 miles and the outer space environment are thought to be significant aids in this problem, the solution to this discrimination problem remains to be demonstrated in theory and practical application. Approximately two years of intensive study and research and development experiments will be required before the feasibility and detailed development plan for an AICBM system can be precisely defined.

C. Surveillance System

    1. High Resolution System

SAMOS follow-ons to achieve greater resolution, greater data rates, and more sophisticated selectivity are receiving continuing study, both within the SAMOS program and elsewhere.

CONFIDENTIAL

This document contains information affecting the national defense of the United States within the meaning of the Espionage Laws, Title 18, U.S.C., Section 793 and 794, the transmission or revelation of which in any manner to an unauthorized person is prohibited by law.

2. Weapon Test Surveillance

This system consists of earth and sun satellites equipped with instruments to detect nuclear explosions at high altitude. In addition, certain ground instrumentation systems are also used. The requirement for this system originates from the 1959 Geneva Nuclear Disarmament Conference.

D. Communications Systems

1. Global Communication Satellite

This system is an operational follow-on of the FLAG system, (National-Survival Communications). Its operational date is estimated to be 1966. Studies to determine the capabilities possible in that time period should be initiated in 1961 or later.

E. Support

1. Advanced Navigation

The earliest version of this system should be used as a navigation aid for persons on the Earth's surface, and might be an outgrowth of the TRANSIT 1 B Program. Eventually, systems of this type might be used as a navigation aid for space vehicles.

2. Re-Supply

Re-supply is a requirement associated with large-scale space operations. Serious system considerations can safely be deferred until 1961 or later, although in the meanwhile this ultimate application should serve to guide DYNA-SOAR and other applicable testing activities.

3. Rescue

A relatively simple satellite with receiver for distress signals and provision for repeating these, together with the location data, would be possible at an early date. Studies to define such a system might be initiated in 1959-60.

WDZR-180

IV-4

CONFIDENTIAL

This document contains information affecting the national defense of the United States within the meaning of the Espionage Laws, Title 18, U.S.C., Section 793 and 794, the transmission or revelation of which in any manner to an unauthorized person is prohibited by law.

4. Transportation-Logistics

    Studies to define a system meeting the transportation-logistics mission requirement might be initiated in 1962.

5. Space Environment Observing and Forecasting System

    The primary purpose of the Space Environmental Observing and Forecasting System is to provide the USAF with an integrated system for observing, processing, and forecasting meteorological, geophysical, and astrophysical phenomena affecting military operations conducted at altitudes above 200,000 feet. A secondary purpose is to observe, from a satellite vehicle, meteorological and environmental conditions below 200,000 feet in support of the "Weather Observing and Forecasting System", GOR 11.

    A development plan prepared in response to GOR 176 proposes to make full use of existing hardware developed under the DISCOVERER, SAMOS, and MIDAS programs. These include the AGENA vehicle, auxiliary power supply, guidance and control, ground to space communications, tracking and acquisition stations, and ground data handling facilities. Use will be made of both the THOR-AGENA combination and the ATLAS-AGENA.

 CONFIDENTIAL

This document contains information affecting the national defense of the United States within the meaning of the Espionage Laws, Title 18, U.S.C., Section 793 and 794, the transmission or revelation of which in any manner to an unauthorized person is prohibited by law.

V. Space Studies

V. SPACE STUDIES

Areas presently under study to investigate directions of future military requirements in the space area are listed below:

A. Strategic Systems

Within this area the following studies have been pursued during the past year or have recently been approved.

1. Recoverable Booster Study (SR 89774)

This is a study to examine the various means of recovering the first stage booster of a space system. The trade-offs between parachute type of recovery and winged vehicle will be examined, for example, and the optimum conditions for the use of various recovery systems will be stipulated.

2. Hypersonic Boost Glide Bombardment-Reconnaissance Studies (SR 126)

Purpose of this study is to examine the military potential of boosting a winged vehicle into a low altitude orbit so that the vehicle is maneuverable by means of aerodynamic forces. The potential of using this concept for bombardment and reconnaissance missions is being explored.

3. Intercontinental Glide Missile (SR 79500)

This is a study to examine the potential of using a lifting type of re-entry warhead which would extend the range and perhaps increase the accuracy of intercontinental missiles. Preliminary calculations indicate that for a given booster the range can be doubled over that of a ballistic missile.

4. Strategic Orbital System (SR 181)

The objective of this study is to examine all the potential military uses of the Earth orbital area. It will take into account all the present systems such as SAMOS and integrate these into a proposed military booster for this regime of space.

This document contains information affecting the national defense of the United States within the meaning of the Espionage Laws, Title 18, U.S.C., Sections 793 and 794, the transmission or revelation of which in any manner to an unauthorized person is prohibited by law.

5. Strategic Lunar System (SR 192)

This is a conceptual study to examine the future military potential of operating upon the surface of the moon and the area around the moon and in cislunar space. The type of systems and their performance parameters are expected to result from this study.

6. Advanced Ballistic Missile Weapon System (SR 199)

Purpose of this study is to examine the potential and feasibility of developing a very large ballistic missile. The payloads under investigation will vary from 20 to 100,000 pounds, and the range required is 8,500 nautical miles.

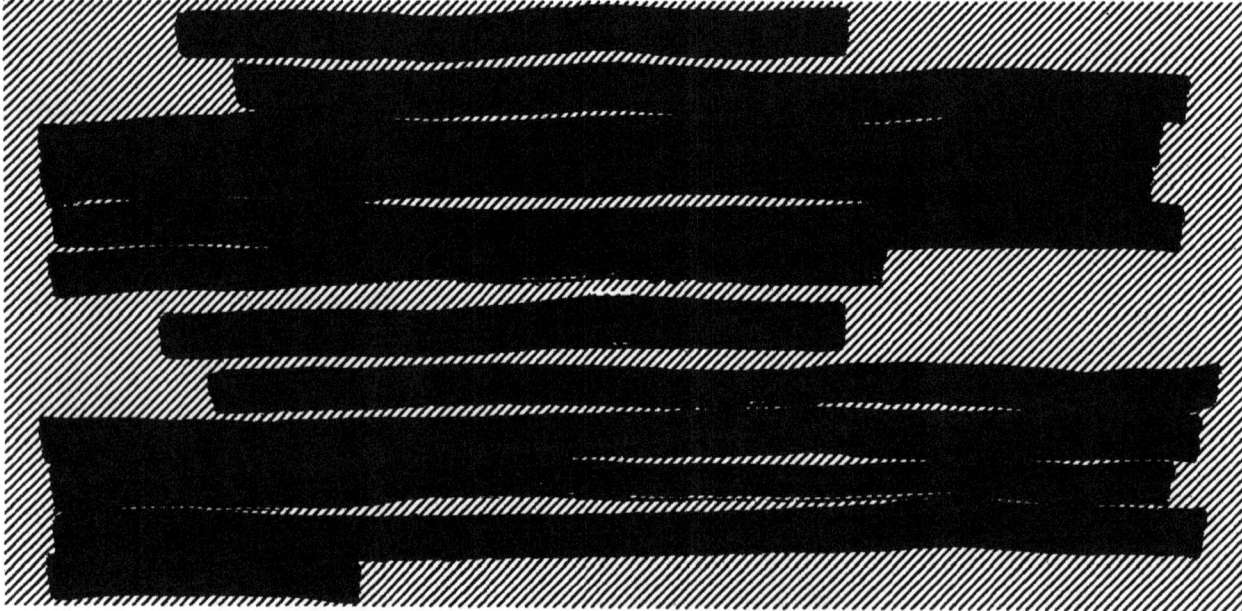

9. Low Altitude Systems Study (No SR Number)

This is an in-house study being conducted at WADC. Purpose is to examine the feasibility of using a satelloid for military missions. A satelloid is a low altitude orbital vehicle which must have a small amount of power applied almost continuously in order to keep it in orbit.

WDZR-180

This document contains information affecting the national defense of the United States within the meaning of the Espionage Laws, Title 18, U.S.C., Section 793 and 794, the transmission or revelation of which in any manner to an unauthorized person is prohibited by law.

BODY-50

10. **Strategic Interplanetary System (SR 182)**

This is a broad conceptual type of study to examine the military potential of operating in the interplanetary area. It is assumed that if the Air Force is able to operate in the lunar area, it will not be a big step to start operations in the interplanetary area. This study may determine the best type of propulsion and guidance systems to use.

B. **Defense Systems**

1. **Advanced Defense Concepts (SR 49758)**

This study will examine the entire defense problems of the future when the Earth-orbiting vehicles may be a threat to this nation. It will examine the means of detecting, neutralizing, and verifying the kill of such vehicles.

2. **Boost-Track Ballistic Missile Defense System (No SR Number)**

Purpose of this study is to examine the means of tracking a ballistic missile during its boost phase. Such tracking is to be accomplished by means of an Earth-orbiting satellite. The system would also have the capability of intercepting and destroying a missile which it detects.

3. **Satellite Inspector System (SR 79998)**

This SR has not been started. However, it is proposed to examine the means of inspecting enemy satellites. It also will examine the various means of neutralizing enemy satellites, and the various means of neutralizing a satellite if it is determined upon inspection to be of a hostile nature.

4. **Satellite Defense Weapon System (SR 79999)**

This is a new study that has not started to date. The objective is to determine the design characteristics of an air-launched satellite interceptor weapon system, including both the requirements of the launching aircraft and the space-borne components of the intercepting payload.

WDZR-180

This document contains information affecting the national defense of the United States within the meaning of the Espionage Laws, Title 18, U.S.C., Section 793 and 794, the transmission or revelation of which in any manner to an unauthorized person is prohibited by law.

C.   Reconnaissance Systems

    1.   Global Surveillance Systems (SR 178)

        The objective of this study is to determine the feasibility of a manned orbital surveillance system. It can be considered a follow-on to the SAMOS project.

    2.   Lunar Observatory (SR 183)

        Purpose of this study is to examine the potential of using a base on the moon for reconnaissance of the Earth and cislunar space. The study is to determine a sound and logical approach to establish and operate such a base on the moon.

D.   Supporting Studies

    1.   Retrieval Concepts (SR 49759)

        The objective of this study is to examine the various means of retrieving space vehicles. It will also determine when certain types of systems such as parachute receivery should be used.

    2.   Advanced Design Trainer (SR 49756)

        This is a study to examine various means of training pilots to operate maneuverable space vehicles.

CONFIDENTIAL

This document contains information affecting the national defense of the United States within the meaning of the Espionage Laws, Title 18, U.S.C., Section 793 and 794, the transmission or revelation of which in any manner to an unauthorized person is prohibited by law.

VI. Test Support Systems

VI. TEST SUPPORT SYSTEMS

There are a number of key research and development support systems which are required to test new designs or techniques which may become part of a new system design or which may be required in applied research programs designed to advance the space technology. Some of these systems or programs are described below.

A. DYNA-SOAR

The objective of the WS-464L (DYNA-SOAR) research program is to develop and demonstrate a piloted winged vehicle capable of carrying man and materials through a sub-orbital, hypersonic boost glide flight regime. The gliders will weigh approximately 9,000 pounds and will achieve up to 50 nautical mile orbits. The boosters will be two-stage variations of either the ATLAS-CENTAUR or the TITAN missiles.

The planned schedule contemplates initial drop tests in 1961, piloted ground launches in early 1963, and global flight late in 1963. The global flight will consist of eastward launch from Cape Canaveral, a circum-navigation of the Earth, and finally a piloted landing at Edwards Air Force Base in California. During the various flights a variety of equipment and techniques will be tested, including environmental system, advanced radar, communications and intelligence systems.

B. WS-609A

The WS-609A system is a modified version of the NASA "SCOUT" four-stage solid propellant vehicle, which is designed to serve as an inexpensive test bed for launching payloads of 100 pounds to altitudes of 4,000 miles and 1,000 pounds to altitudes of 1,000 miles. The system serves as a test bed for component and subsystem tests and special research tests. The initial system will be ready for limited use, concurrent with vehicle development testing, in mid-1960.

WDZR-180

VI-1

This document contains information affecting the national defense of the United States within the meaning of the Espionage Laws, Title 18, U.S.C., Section 793 and 794, the transmission or revelation of which in any manner to an unauthorized person is prohibited by law.

D. Re-entry Test Vehicle

An advanced re-entry test vehicle program is being considered. Objectives of the advanced RTV program would be to provide a hypersonic re-entry test environment for the testing of advanced low-cost ablating materials for ICBM nose cone, the development of low-temperature ablation materials for lifting type re-entry vehicle heat protection, and for providing a test environment for the development of heat protection of re-entry vehicles operating at re-entry velocities up to 30,000 ft/sec. This re-entry test vehicle program is desired to provide for the development of suitable heat protection materials for uses in the various space missions that involve re-entry.

E. Hypersonic Lifting Re-entry

A program of study, research, and demonstration of hypersonic lifting re-entry vehicles in a range of designs involving moderately low ratios of lift-to-drag is being considered. Studies have been completed by a number of agencies. A rocket vehicle test program could be instituted to obtain actual test data on scale models of the desired vehicles under hypersonic re-entry conditions similar to the applications anticipated.

WDZR-180

CONFIDENTIAL VI-2

This document contains information affecting the national defense of the United States within the meaning of the Espionage Laws, Title 18, U.S.C., Section 793 and 794, the transmission or revelation of which in any manner to an unauthorized person is prohibited by law.

Early phases of this program can be performed relatively easily with ballistic trajectories utilizing the instrumentation facilities available in the Atlantic Missile Range. Later tests should involve re-entry from a low altitude orbit and should include test and evaluation of terminal control, guidance, and communication schemes, as well as obtaining aerodynamic data and vehicle design evaluations.

F. High-Altitude Sounding Rockets

1. JAVELIN-JOURNEYMAN

These are solid propellant high altitude research vehicles. JAVELIN was developed for sounding rocket support of the original ARGUS high-altitude nuclear test. JOURNEYMAN is now under development for instrumentation support of ▮▮▮▮▮ nuclear tests. JAVELIN has a 750-mile altitude capability with about 100-pounds payload. JOURNEYMAN has a 1,700-mile capability with a 100-pound payload. The fourth stage of the rocket is spin stabilized; however, the instrumentation head is de-spun after fourth-stage separation. The first three stages are aerodynamically stabilized. The concept is to provide relatively inexpensive, readily movable sounding rocket support.

2. JAGUAR

This is an air-launched sounding rocket development presently undergoing development at AFSWC. The aircraft used is a B-57 which utilizes vertical launch. This system is an outgrowth of the original NACA effort which was taken over by the Air Force. Basic advantages for such sounding rocket systems are that it provides flexibility and relatively low-cost research and development effort. Launchings in polar regions are contemplated at present. The JAGUAR has a 500-mile altitude capability within the order of 50 to 100 pounds. The potential of a B-58 carrier with a better sounding rocket capability is under study.

The JOURNEYMAN and JAGUAR programs, except for motor fabrication, are in-house efforts and are launched by Air Force crews.

This document contains information affecting the national defense of the United States within the meaning of the Espionage Laws, Title 18, U.S.C., Section 793 and 794, the transmission or revelation of which in any manner to an unauthorized person is prohibited by law.

VII. Analysis of the Program and

Its Systems

VII. ANALYSIS OF THE PROGRAM AND ITS SYSTEMS

The evolution of a weapon system was outlined in general terms in Section I, above. Sections II through VI contain statements of operational requirements, descriptions of systems that might fulfill the requirements and system studies and test support programs that have a bearing on the selection, design and development of the systems. It is of interest to summarize the space program schedule and the space systems characteristics, and to discuss the problem of program analysis and system design.

A. Space Program Schedule, and System Priorities

Table VII-1 contains a schedule of the space system programs. This schedule includes those systems which were discussed in Sections III and IV and which are under development or study, or might be considered, for fulfilling a requirement. The table indicates the study phase and the active programming phase, and approximate first launch and operational dates, where a rough estimate or, in some cases, pure speculation was possible.

The operational requirements have been stated. Systems to fulfill the requirements have been described and the schedule and status of the systems have been summarized. In two instances (THOR and ATLAS) the systems are operational. A few are in the advanced design stage. Others have been through operational concept studies and preliminary design analysis, but the majority of the advanced systems are in the early study phase and have yet to reach the preliminary design analysis stage.

There are two good reasons for this situation. First, to date, no one has established a military space program with sufficient clarity in scope and priority to permit scheduling and funding of the detailed system analysis and design effort on advanced systems. Secondly, the advanced technology required for the understanding and development of such systems, and the magnitude of expenditures to

WDZR-180

VII-1

 CONFIDENTIAL

This document contains information affecting the national defense of the United States within the meaning of the Espionage Laws, Title 18, U.S.C., Section 793 and 794, the transmission or revelation of which in any manner to an unauthorized person is prohibited by law.

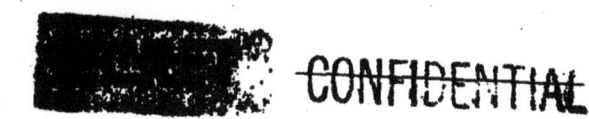

be anticipated on advanced systems argue against the initiation of extensive development effort on a number of systems until a priority is established. This situation is not likely to change in the near future insofar as the advanced systems are concerned, for we are feeling our way in the new science of astronautics.

With this in mind, a priority must be established among those near-term systems (1960-70) and they must be analyzed thoroughly. Development plans must be prepared and development initiated. At this time, those systems which should receive the most active support appear to be, in order of priority, the following:

Ballistic Missile Defense System -

Intensive study, measurements and component development on a systems basis, directed toward selection and development of complete system.

Missile Attack Alarm -

Completion of MIDAS development and an immediate, parallel effort to develop and advanced attack alarm system to be part of the Ballistic Missile Defense System and to alert the deterrent forces and civil defense agencies.

Surveillance -

Completion of SAMOS and an immediate parallel effort on an advanced surveillance system.

Communications -

Completion of SAC-Polar Satellite, including the advanced version, and on parallel basis, initiation of development on FLAG (National Survival Communications Satellite).

WDZR-180

VII-2

SECRET CONFIDENTIAL

This document contains information affecting the national defense of the United States within the meaning of the Espionage Laws, Title 18, U.S.C., Section 793 and 794, the transmission or revelation of which in any manner to an unauthorized person is prohibited by law.

Satellite Defense -

Completion of development of ground-launched
intercept and inspection system and parallel
effort on extending capability of SPACE TRACK
ground-based satellite tracking and cataloguing
system to skin-track and catalogue all non-
cooperative satellites passing over U.S.

Manned Space System -

Completion of DYNA-SOAR Research Program;
and intense study directed toward development
of a manned multi-purpose space vehicle for
both defense and offense applications.

Two systems not included in the above priority list are the Outer
Space Weapon Test Surveillance System and the Outer Space Weapons
Test System, both of which hold a priority to be determined nationally.

The above outlined development effort must be accompanied by
an extensive advanced systems study program which utilizes industry
capabilities and talent to a maximum. The ARDC Study Requirements
program, which includes the studies listed in Section V, above, can
produce and guide these studies if the SR program is more carefully
directed and coordinated with space system development.

Associated with the systems development and advanced system
study must be an effort to correlate subsystem and major component
development of the many systems wherever possible, and to initiate
the necessary advanced research and development in critical areas,
which require a decided advance in technology. Such correlation
requires an analysis of the systems involved to determine the operational concept and design f█████████ ticular importance is the

This document contains information affecting the national defense of the United States within the meaning of the Espionage Laws, Title

development and test of lifting re-entry vehicles and recoverable boosters.

B. Operational Characteristics and System Specifications

Table VII-2 is a summary of system specifications or characteristics for some of the listed space systems. In some cases these
specifications are reasonably firm, in others they are very crude
estimates. Both this table and Table VII-1 are intended to be based
on data obtained from established weapon system programs, from design
studies and system concept studies. In its present form the data is
somewhat preliminary but will suffice to show what is being attempted
in the long range plan.

The analysis of a system in sufficient detail to provide
operational characteristics and preliminary design specifications is
usually accomplished in development plan studies and in design studies
made subsequent to development plan approval. It is intended that the
effort associated with the SPADE Plan will promote analysis of the
selected space systems on an accelerated and coordinated basis in
accordance with the priority accepted and established. This will
permit an expansion of the table and refinement of the data now in the
table.

In the section which follows, we will discuss the use of this
data and the space program schedule in analyzing future Air Force
space booster requirements.

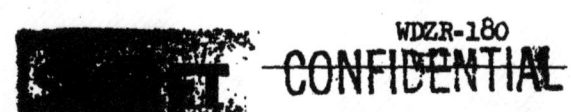

This document contains information affecting the national defense of the United States within the meaning of the Espionage Laws, Title 18, U.S.C., Section 793 and 794, the transmission or revelation of which in any manner to an unauthorized person is prohibited by law. BODY-61

CONFIDENTIAL

CONFIDENTIAL

BODY-62

VIII. Subsystem Correlation and Development

VIII. SUBSYSTEM CORRELATION AND DEVELOPMENT

Section VII discussed space program analysis and the necessity for an orderly program of systems development accompanied by advanced systems studies. The need to correlate major component requirements and promote technological advancement in critical component areas was emphasized.

Timely development of the required space systems is a strong reason for a coordinated technological advancement program. A more urgent reason is saving of dollars. The cost of space system development and production is the real governing factor in the kind and numbers of space weapons which the U.S. may put into operation. To get the most for our dollar, we must not only establish priorities but also must take steps to minimize the tremendous expenditures per system.

One big step is the correlation of requirements and coordination of major component development wherever possible. Appendix "D" presents some representative areas of technical development and basic research which could contribute to future weapon systems. The list is not comprehensive in its present form nor does it indicate priorities or areas of greatest potential payoff. It is intended as a starting point for correlation of research and development efforts with space weapon system requirements.

All the technical disciplines listed in Appendix "D" must be considered in detail for sound planning of their place in new weapon systems. These areas include communication, radar, computers, tracking, guidance, power supplies, rocket engines, booster vehicles, controls, reentry, materials, propellants, low-thrust propulsion, and others. An eventual objective of the SPADE plan is to relate these technical areas to weapon system requirements.

 CONFIDENTIAL

This document contains information affecting the national defense of the United States within the meaning of the Espionage Laws, Title 18, U.S.C., Section 793 and 794, the transmission or revelation of which in any manner to an unauthorized person is prohibited by law.

CONFIDENTIAL

An example of the technique proposed is the analysis of Air Force space booster development requirements which is included as Appendix "C". This analysis includes a proposed development program for this major subsystem. A brief look at the approach to this ten year (1960-1970) booster requirements analysis is of interest.

A space booster is any particular combination of propulsion vehicle stages which will place a specified payload on a particular flight path. As such it includes all integral vehicle subsystems (e.g., propulsion, guidance and control, internal power, and associated tracking/communications equipment).

A. Operational Concept and System Characteristics

The degree to which a future booster can be defined is dependent on the degree that the payload and flight path can be defined. The first operational techniques for space are only now being demonstrated. From these and from experience with ballistic missiles, reasonably accurate estimates of concepts and characteristics can be made for some near-term systems. These data, which were obtained from individual program design and development plans, are assembled in Table VII-2. Further extrapolation by extension to systems in the advanced study area is necessary for extension through the 1966-70 period. Correlation with the required time period may be made by reference to the Space Program schedule in Table VII-1.

B. State-of-the-Art

Once an estimate of booster requirements by system is assembled, it is necessary then to look at the present and projected booster capability. Booster vehicles available now or in the immediate future are tabulated in Table C-1 of Appendix "C". These boosters are based primarily upon the use of ballistic missile hardware with slight modification and the addition of appropriate upper stages.

SECRET   CONFIDENTIAL

This document contains information affecting the national defense of the United States within the meaning of the Espionage Laws, Title 18, U.S.C., Section 793 and 794; the transmission or revelation of which in any manner to an unauthorized person is prohibited by law.

It then becomes necessary to look carefully at the future possibilities in space vehicles, including the research programs in progress, the advanced studies and state-of-the-art improvement programs in propulsion, guidance, and other pertinent areas.

C.   A Recommended Program

When the future booster requirements are assembled and the forecast of technology is known, the proposed program may be configured. A compromise is necessary because selection of a limited number of discrete booster systems, with associated research requirements, is dictated by the high cost of their development and production. This compromise does not penalize the individual systems, because the selection is coordinated and timely and appropriate adjustments may be made in system planning.

The resulting proposed Air Force booster program and associated research program are outlined and discussed in Appendix "C". One very critical need in this area is the development of an economical booster which could make certain very expensive space weapon programs feasible as well as reduce the overall cost of the space program. Approaches include the design of a recoverable booster and/or major design improvements in non-recoverable boosters.

D.   Future Analysis

It is intended that, with the cooperation and participation of interested laboratories and agencies, and through cooperation with industry, all of the major space component areas will be thoroughly analyzed. This analysis should uncover critical areas, and selected component research and development programs may be initiated to support systems development.

WDZR-180

VIII-3

CONFIDENTIAL

This document contains information affecting the national defense of the United States within the meaning of the Espionage Laws, Title 18, U.S.C., Section 793 and 794, the transmission or revelation of which in any manner to an unauthorized person is prohibited by law.

IX. Conclusions

IX. CONCLUSIONS

The following conclusions are based on the SPADE Plan and the study and effort associated with its preparation.

The SPADE Plan can serve as an official planning guide in the Air Force Space System Development Program, to assist the decision process and in coordinating and ordering development effort. The initial report is preliminary, but will serve as the framework for continuing study. It will assist using commands in defining operational requirements, and centers and laboratories in analyzing development requirements and in prosecuting the development program. Through the cooperation and participation of interested commands and agencies, detailed analysis of each of the required systems may be accomplished, and the report may be refined and extended.

A definite requirement exists for an official statement of system requirements and a development priority among systems. The requirements outlined in Section II and the priority stated in Section VII may suffice as a starting point for this action.

WDZR-180

IX-1

 CONFIDENTIAL

This document contains information affecting the national defense of the United States within the meaning of the Espionage Laws, Title 18, U.S.C., Section 793 and 794, the transmission or revelation of which in any manner to an unauthorized person is prohibited by law.

Appendix A - Definition of Terms

APPENDIX A

DEFINITIONS OF TERMS

The following selected definitions are pertinent to an understanding of the SPADE document:

Booster -

The vehicle system designed to transport the payload into space, place it on the proper orbits or trajectories, and control its flight path, attitude and environment thereafter as required by the mission of the payload. Includes propulsion, guidance and control and associated telemetry, vehicle structural units, and primary auxiliary power sources, as well as the necessary ground environment incidental to launch and guidance.

Major component -

A combination of units or parts that together may be functionally independent of, or an independent entity within a complete operating subsystem, but providing a self-contained function necessary for proper subsystem and/or system operation.

Mission -

A specific assignment, service or duty to be accomplished by a person, organization, office, detachment or the like, with the object of contributing functionally to an overall objective.

Payload -

The functional package including sensors, instrumentation and supporting bracketry which must be placed and maintained in the appropriate space environment in order to perform the primary mission of the space flight.

WDZR-180

A-1

This document contains information affecting the national defense of the United States within the meaning of the Espionage Laws, Title 18, U.S.C., Section 793 and 794, the transmission or revelation of which in any manner to an unauthorized person is prohibited by law.

Plan -

> The detailed approach or methodology to be employed in
> attaining specified program objectives, includes summar-
> ization of physical characteristics, the operational concepts
> involved and the resources needed for successful accom -
> plishment of the objective.
>
>   or:
>
> The design, method, or scheme for accomplishing a mission
> or reaching an objective.

Space system -

> An integrated relationship of all subdivisions of an operating
> complex including checkout/servicing equipment, together
> with associated personnel; all aligned to establish proper
> functional continuity towards the successful performance of
> a defined task or tasks.

Subsystem -

> A single module, or a combination of modules, plus independ-
> ent components that contribute to modular functions, all inter-
> connected and interrelated within a system and performing a
> specific system function.

System integration -

> The process of insuring that all elements of the entire system
> will properly perform their functions, are mutually compatible
> and are available in a timely manner.

Weapon system -

> Equipment, skills, and techniques, the composite of which
> forms an instrument of combat. The complete weapon system
> includes all related equipment, material, services and
> personnel required solely for the operation of the air vehicle,
> or other major element of the system, so that the instrument
> of combat becomes a self-sufficient unit of striking power in
> its intended operational environment.

WDZR - 180

A-2

 CONFIDENTIAL

This document contains information affecting the national defense of the United States within the meaning of the Espionage Laws, Title 18, U.S.C., Section 793 and 794, the transmission or revelation of which in any manner to an unauthorized person is prohibited by law.

BODY-73

Appendix B - References

APPENDIX B

REFERENCES

A selected list of references applicable to the systems discussed in the SPADE plan are included below. This list is not intended to be inclusive, but does list development plans and other documents of principal interest.

Offense

THOR (WS-315A)	Development Plan GOR 50	August 1959
ATLAS (WS-107A-1)	Development Plan GOR 104	November 1959 (In process)
TITAN (WS-107A-2)	Development Plan GOR 104	August 1959
MINUTEMAN (WS-133A)	Development Plan GOR 171	August 1959

Defense

MIDAS (Missile Attack Alarm)	Development Plan	30 January 1959
SAINT (Satellite Interceptor)	Development Plan GOR 170 SR 187	10 August 1959

Surveillance

SAMOS	Development Plan GOR 80	30 January 1959

WDZR-180

B-1

This document contains information affecting the national defense of the United States within the meaning of the Espionage Laws, Title 18, U.S.C., Section 793 and 794, the transmission or revelation of which in any manner to an unauthorized person is prohibited by law.

BODY-75

 CONFIDENTIAL

Communications

COURIER	Development Plan ARPA Order 17-59	November 1959 (In process)
STEER) (Polar Satellite))) SAC POLAR Satellite)) TACKLE/DECREE) (24-hour Comm.) Satellite))	Development Plan	December 1958 (New plans in process)
FLAG (National Survival)	Development Plan	27 July 1959

Support

TIROS (Weather Observation)	Development Plan GOR 176	30 June 1959
TRANSIT (Navigation)	Development Plan	(In process)

Test Systems

WS-609A	Development Plan System Directive 609A	18 May 1959 5 February 1959
DYNA-SOAR	Development Plan GOR 92 SR 126 SR 181	25 November 1957
OSWT	Development Plan	1 September 1959

 SECRET CONFIDENTIAL

This document contains information affecting the national defense of the United States within the meaning of the Espionage Laws, Title 18, U.S.C., Section 793 and 794, the transmission or revelation of which in any manner to an unauthorized person is prohibited by law.

Appendix C - Booster Development

Requirements

CONFIDENTIAL

APPENDIX C

AIR FORCE MILITARY BOOSTER DEVELOPMENT PROGRAM

A. INTRODUCTION

A space booster is the vehicle system designed to transport the payload into space, place it on the proper orbits or trajectories, and control its flight path, attitude and environment thereafter as required by the mission of the payload. It includes propulsion, guidance and control and associated telemetry, vehicle structural units, and primary auxiliary power sources, as well as the necessary ground environment incidental to launch and guidance.

The objectives of this analysis are to:

     (i) Establish general criteria as a basis for planning a military booster development program.

     (ii) Review military booster needs.

     (iii) Define the booster development program which will most economically fill military needs.

B. BASIC CRITERIA

Space systems are by their very nature complex and expensive. As will be seen later, military system needs are rapidly being defined and expanded. Extrapolation of present-day costs indicates that, under present concepts, this nation cannot afford to develop all the systems which will be needed. In some cases where high launch rates are required to make a system effective, the cost of one system alone may be prohibitive. The United States must maintain a balanced effective defense posture against attack. Therefore, criteria for planning space system and booster development should be based on an over-riding need for reduction in cost.

Methods for reducing costs in terms of dollars per pound of payload are currently under investigation. This analysis is based on the fact that the major costs presently involved in the operation of ballistic missiles and space vehicle systems are hardware manufacturing costs and those associated with launch operations. A long range objective should be to evolve booster designs which make maximum use of economical materials

CONFIDENTIAL

This document contains information affecting the national defense of the United States within the meaning of the Espionage Laws, Title 18, U.S.C., Section 793 and 794, the transmission or revelation of which in any manner to an unauthorized person is prohibited by law.

and construction techniques. Checkout and count-down operations must be simplified to eliminate complex support equipment and facilities as well as reduce the operational manpower needed.

Reduction in development costs can be accomplished by developing boosters, subsystems, and stages which are usable for a variety of missions with a minimum of modification. The possibility of combining payloads to perform more than one type of mission is also attractive. New booster and subsystem developments should be carefully planned to insure growth potential and direct applicability to later requirements insofar as they can be defined. This would enable a minimum of new booster, stage, and subsystem development programs.

Reduction in production costs could be achieved in three ways. The ability to use major portions of the same booster for different payload and trajectory requirements results in greater gross production with a commensurate reduction in cost per unit. Possible recovery and re-use of major portions of the booster vehicle could result in substantial savings. The savings actually obtained in stage recovery depend on the balance between the cost of recovery and the cost of a new stage. They will be a function of the number of different missions the same stage will be used for since this will determine the number of launches over which the cost of a recovery system can be amortized. They will also depend on the ability of the recovered stage to be used again with a minimum of inspection, repair, and checkout.

Reduction in the cost of launch operations could best be obtained by reducing the ground facility and support equipment requirements. Decrease in subsystems complexity would, in addition, tend to simplify checkout and count-down operations. This would reduce technical manhour requirements as well as provide more efficient launch-facility utilization.

The ever increasing need for greater performance and versatility of booster systems appears in conflict with the above discussion. Analysis of staged weapon systems indicates that overall performance, and versa-

This document contains information affecting the national defense of the United States within the meaning of the Espionage Laws, Title 18, U.S.C., Section 793 and 794, the transmission or revelation of which in any manner to an unauthorized person is prohibited by law.

tility of booster vehicles are most sensitive to the design and performance characteristics of the last stage. Since the final stage is also the smallest, it is easier to handle, and involves smaller weights of hardware. In order to make maximum use of the larger stages, a greater variety of last stage designs appear to be needed. The need for maximum performance on the more stringent missions dictates that emphasis should be on the use of highest-energy propellants in the last stage. This does not necessarily obviate the continued need for versatile work-horse stages with more moderate-performance propellants which are logistically easier to handle.

A final consideration is based upon the fact that, at present and for the next few years, our major space booster capabilities rely on existing ballistic missile hardware. Space was not considered a practical reality when ballistic missile development was initiated. The state of our technology and the nature of the threat also made cost a secondary objective. As a result, present space vehicles using ballistic missile stages are expensive items at any production rate. Present booster vehicles with high-energy upper stages appear sufficient for immediate needs but order-of-magnitude increases in capability are required in the near future. Development of new high-energy upper stages for use with ballistic missile stages should be conducted with their possible applicability to later, more optimum, space boosters in mind.

In summary, general criteria for planning a booster development program for space vehicles must be based on an overriding need for reduction in cost per pound of payload. These criteria are:

2.   (i) Stages and boosters should be sized and developed to accommodate a maximum number of mission/payload requirements with a minimum of modification.

(ii) New stages developed should include a reasonable growth potential and be adaptable for use with larger follow-on booster vehicle developments.. "Dead-end" development should be avoided.

(iii) Large stage development should be based on maximum simplification of design, fabrication techniques, and launch operations. Ruggedness

This document contains information affecting the national defense of the United States within the meaning of the Espionage Laws, Title 18, U.S.C., Section 793 and 794, the transmission or revelation of which in any manner to an unauthorized person is prohibited by law.

BODY-80

and simplicity at the expense of over-all stage performance will be acceptable if significant economies result.

(iv) Maximum performance and sophistication should be planned for the development of final booster stages.

(v) The broadest approach to long lead-time development should apply to final stage subsystem development.

C. MILITARY BOOSTER NEEDS

The degree to which a future space booster can be defined is dependent on the degree that the payload and flight path involved can be defined. Intensive study and analysis is being performed to establish the various military potentialities of space. However, demonstration of operational techniques for initial military space systems is just starting. Not enough is now known about true space environments and a well-planned and conducted program of space exploration is needed before many presently indicated military possibilities can be confirmed and weapon systems defined in detail.

The extent to which missions and payloads can be defined is a function of how far analysis extends into the future. This means that booster needs for the near future can be quite definitive. However, exact definition of booster needs ten years hence is impossible and, in fact, unnecessary.

Table 1 lists presently available and immediate future space booster vehicles based on ballistic missile stages. Approximate mission payload capabilities are also indicated. Maximum immediate capabilities range from about 6,000 pounds in a 300 nautical mile orbit to about 400 pounds in 24-hour orbit. The first need is to achieve maximum practical use from the existing ICBM stages. With no major structural modification it appears that appropriate upper stages using high-energy propellants can provide capabilities up to about 8,000 pounds in a 300 nautical mile orbit and about 1,600 pounds in 24-hour orbit. The most attractive vehicles of this type are illustrated in Figure 1. This will be sufficient to accommodate systems presently approved for development and many follow-on requirements. However,

WDZR-180

C-4

This document contains information affecting the national defense of the United States within the meaning of the Espionage Laws, Title 18, U.S.C., Section 793 and 794, the transmission or revelation of which in any manner to an unauthorized person is prohibited by law.

BODY-81

performance requirements have been defined for the 1963-64 time period which need substantially greater mission/payload capabilities. Some of the major systems which have been defined and their present status are as follows:

(i) FLAG - National survival SAC communication system. This requires up to 4,000 pounds in a 19,400 nautical mile equatorial orbit. A development plan has been submitted.

(ii) WHITE SAINT - Unmanned satellite inspection and/or negation system. This requires about 3,500 pounds in orbits up to 2,000 nautical miles. A development plan has been submitted.

(iii) DYNA-SOAR I - Hypersonic glide vehicle. This requires a 7,500-10,000 pound payload launched into a 50 nautical mile apogee glide path. This program is awaiting final approval.

(iv) Advanced Ballistic Missile (GOR 180). This requires payloads of up to 20,000 pounds delivered over an 8,500 nautical mile range. Detailed system studies are being performed.

Booster stage requirements are firm for most of these systems. The exact booster configuration which will be developed to accommodate them, however, will be determined by the first system or systems approved for development and their relative priorities. It appears that a first stage of about 800,000 pounds thrust and a second stage of about 200,000 pounds thrust with appropriate third stages can best provide the desired performance. For instance, addition of a 30,000 pound thrust stage using high-energy propellants will more than satisfy requirements for the FLAG system.

For the 1964-66 time period, requirements are less clear and more subject to revision. Military mission/payload requirements which can be described range from realistic approximations to pure guess. In addition, there are distinct possibilities of now undefined requirements due to rapidly advancing technologies, the results of studies now being performed, and the possibilities of combining some payload requirements. Some of the high-

This document contains information affecting the national defense of the United States within the meaning of the Espionage Laws, Title 18, U.S.C., Section 793 and 794, the transmission or revelation of which in any manner to an unauthorized person is prohibited by law.

BODY-82

payload system needs which appear more clearly defined are as follows:

(i)   Advanced FLAG - 24 hour military communications satellite.

(ii) BLUE SAINT - Manned satellite inspection and/or negation system.

(iii) DYNA-SOAR II - Manned orbital boost-glide bombardment/reconnaissance system.

(iv) Advanced Ballistic Missile (SR 199)

(v)   AICBM - Satellite-borne ICBM negation system.

In addition, studies are underway and possible systems have been investigated to varying degrees for advanced reconnaissance satellites, satellite bombardment systems, advanced missile detection, tracking, and negation systems, and even manned space stations or lunar bases.

By the time a decision can be made (around 1964-66) to initiate stage development for the 1967-70 time period, much more will be known about space and the military potential of operating therein. Possibilities demonstrated by then for nuclear or other new propulsive means may change the current outlook for chemical propulsion. The possibility of assembly-in-space techniques or orbit rendezvous and refueling techniques may make larger payloads more practical through the use of several smaller boosters instead of one giant booster. A recent study performed under ARPA Order 93-59 and based on extrapolations of present day experience indicates that orbit-refueling, using "tanker" vehicles and chemical propulsion, might be more economical than the use of single very large chemical systems or even advanced nuclear systems. The only safe statement which can be made today concerning booster requirements for the 1967-70 time period is that missions will be more stringent, flight paths will be more complex, and payload weight requirements will be much larger. Not all new systems under study now will be developed. Some may be combined, at least as far as basic payload configuration is concerned.

D. RECOMMENDED PROGRAM

There are two basic approaches to filling future space booster needs. One is to base plans on extrapolations of present-day technology and the

This document contains information affecting the _____ States within the meaning of the Espionage Laws, Title 18, U.S.C., Section 793 and 794, the transmission or revelation of which in any manner to an unauthorized person is prohibited by law.

assumption of propulsion, secondary power, guidance, and control, and structural subsystems similar to those in existence. This is the conservative approach. Unfortunately, this approach results in booster vehicles, stages, and subsystems whose cost appears to prohibit development of the numbers and kinds of systems which appear to be needed.

There is need for an economic breakthrough in the development of large chemical booster stages. Present analyses indicate that the following characteristics are required.

1. Simplicity

This requirement dictates a minimum system complexity and number of operating components. Design simplicity indicates a preference for pressurized feed systems, the use of a minimum number of propulsion units, elimination of mechanical vector control, if possible, and a minimum of components requiring close tolerance manufacturing or exotic materials.

2. Ruggedness

Stages should be designed for rough handling and possible stage recovery and re-use.

3. Reliability

Design, fabrication and operational procedures should be directed toward maximum probability of mission success.

4. Simple Pre-launch Checkout

There is need for drastic improvement in checkout procedures and reduction of associated launch equipment needs.

Means for accomplishing the above objectives have been investigated. Preliminary results indicate the feasibility of a completely new approach to meeting stage requirements for large military boosters. Two new stage design concepts have been evolved. One, designated "Phoenix",

SECRET CONFIDENTIAL

This document contains information affecting the national defense of the United States within the meaning of the Espionage Laws, Title 18, U.S.C., Section 793 and 794, the transmission or revelation of which in any manner to an unauthorized person is prohibited by law.

applies to high-thrust stage requirements. The other, designated "Aurora", applies to altitude stages using high-energy propellants. Further analysis of both concepts is continuing and initial developments to prove weapon system potential are proposed. They will be outlined in greater detail in the following discussion of the over-all recommended booster development program.

Requirements for the 1962-63 time period must rely on the conventional approach to high-thrust stage development. An over-all program must be planned commensurate with the criteria outlined in Section B, using conventional chemical stage design. This is in the full realization that at some later date, currently thought to be three to six years hence, major decisions will be needed based on progress made with the Phoenix concept.

Figure 2 illustrates, by a cross-hatched band, how payload needs are expected to increase using a 300 nautical mile orbit capability for comparison. The width of the band is indicative of the degree of uncertainty existing concerning these needs. The diagrammatic vehicles shown are only examples of booster vehicles possible with the propulsion systems proposed for development. This is in recognition of the fact that stage size is largely determined by the propulsion system. Actual vehicles developed will depend on the individual military weapon systems approved for development.

The specific program recommended in the high-thrust booster area is delineated in Figure 3. Propulsion and propellant tankage requirements have an overriding effect on booster size and thrust requirements so it is outlined in that context. The need to insure success in attaining advanced capabilities in space dictate propulsion backup approaches due to the somewhat unpredictable nature of advanced rocket propulsion development programs. The need for economy and the rapidity of technological advances dictates close monitorship of the over-all program and the ability to make rapid technical and program decisions. Some of the major decisions we presently foresee are indicated by numbered boxes in Figure 3.

CONFIDENTIAL

This document contains information affecting the national defense of the United States within the meaning of the Espionage Laws, Title 18, U.S.C.; Section 793 and 794, the transmission or revelation of which in any manner to an unauthorized person is prohibited by law.

There are two possible approaches to achieving an 800,000 pound thrust first stage for the 1962-63 time period. One is to take advantage of the ballistic missile program and the uprating of the basic LR 87 engine to 200,000 pounds thrust using storable propellants. The other is to use the LR 109 basic engine currently rated at 300,000 to 400,000 pounds of thrust. This engine does not have the extensive development testing already achieved with the LR 87. However, it does have growth potential to over 500,000 pounds thrust and is simpler, using fewer engines in cluster to provide the thrust needed in vehicles for this period and for follow-on vehicle stages. It is recommended for primary development toward an 800,000 pound thrust booster stage. The LR 87 is recommended as a primary conventional development toward an altitude engine for the required second stage and as a backup development toward the first stage requirement. As is indicated in Figure 3, two major decisions should be possible about one year after initiation of the program. First, it should be possible to decide on a single approach to meeting 800,000 pounds thrust stage requirements. Second, detailed technical and cost analyses performed in the meantime should indicate whether the LR 87 altitude engine should be paired to fill later 400,000 pound thrust second stage requirements or whether an altitude version of the LR 109 engine would be more desirable.

The F-1 (one million pound thrust) engine development, currently under NASA sponsorship should be oriented toward filling conventional first-stage requirements for military boosters of the 1964-66 time period and beyond. It should be recognized, however, that the thrust developed by this engine is more than three times that of other engines in existence. The classical problems involved with the scaling up of rocket engines (combustion instability, heat transfer, vibration, injector design) may offer complications yet undetermined. Well over a year of aggressive development and test are needed before systems development planning can be based on a firm engine development schedule.

The basic LR 109 engine in a cluster of three or four can provide the needed stage propulsion. It is considered the best backup to producing

WDZR-180

C-9

CONFIDENTIAL

This document contains information affecting the national defense of the United States within the meaning of the Espionage Laws, Title 18, U.S.C., Section 793 and 794, the transmission or revelation of which in any manner to an unauthorized person is prohibited by law.

1,500,000 pounds of thrust with conventional engines. As is indicated in Figure 3, a decision should be possible within two years as to which propulsion system should be selected for stage-oriented development.

The Saturn booster, currently a responsibility of the NASA, is a more costly and less desirable approach to filling high-thrust booster requirements in the 1962-63 time period. It is a dead-end development as far as follow-on requirements are concerned. However its performance capabilities are expected to be roughly comparable to those of boosters using the 800,000 pound thrust stage described above. It is therefore considered a backup program for filling first-stage requirements in the 1962-63 time period.

Since booster stages for the 1962-63 time period and beyond will be specifically intended for space weapon systems, the primary design considerations will be economy and reliability. Maximum economy of operation involves recovery and reuse of first stages and, possibly, second stages. The most promising approach to acceptable reliability is through simplicity and standardized well-developed components. Together these requirements dictate development of a new type of first stage which exists today only as a design concept which has been given the name Phoenix.

At present the most attractive Phoenix configuration is based upon the use of a pressure-fed propulsion system using liquid oxygen and liquid hydrogen, an uncooled ablating plug nozzle and segmented combustion chambers. Rugged tanks would be designed specifically to facilitate stage recovery and re-use. High-energy propellant performance and continuous optimum expansion characteristics would offset the use of lower chamber pressures. Combustion chamber development in single segment size would permit flexible engine sizing by choice of number of segments. If this particular design continues to be attractive after further investigation, the Phoenix program could start quickly by initiating sybsystem development without commitment to a stage size. Subsystem work would include a chamber-segment test program, tank pressurization tech-

WDZR-180

C-10

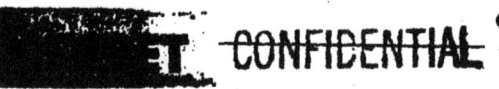 CONFIDENTIAL

This document contains information affecting the national defense of the United States within the meaning of the Espionage Laws, Title 18, U.S.C., Section 793 and 794, the transmission or revelation of which in any manner to an unauthorized person is prohibited by law.

nique investigation, plug nozzle flow analysis and experimentation, and ablating material tests. A corollary stage recovery and reuse program to include analysis and demonstration phases would be essential. The TITAN first stage is an attractive stage for development of recovery and reuse techniques.

Figure 3 indicates that aggressive practical investigation of the Phoenix concept should be initiated now. At such time that successful development of high-thrust stages has been proven feasible under this concept, a major decision must be made as is indicated in the figure. The goals of the Phoenix program are such that their achievement could result in a phasing out of the conventional approach to high thrust stage development. Figure 4 illustrates the present concept of what a Phoenix booster vehicle would look like. For illustrative purposes only, consecutive 800,000 pound and three-million pound thrust stage developments were presumed.

Another approach to simplification of high thrust stages which should be considered is through the use of solid propellants. The present MINUTEMAN, POLARIS, and PERSHING programs will provide a family of stages with thrusts ranging up to over 100,000 pounds. Use of these motors will very likely be found in specific weapon system programs. However, the potential of solid propellants for very high thrust applications cannot be determined until the results of the present high-impulse state-of-the-art program are known and detailed systems cost analyses have been completed involving production, handling, performance, and operational parameters. The state-of-the-art investigation should be continued until the potentialities of very large solid propellant motors can be determined.

Emphasis in upper stage development should be on the use of high-energy propellants. While technological improvement in other subsystem areas such as guidance, secondary power, stabilization and control should be rapid also, propulsion development is still expected to be the controlling factor for stage sizing and availability. As is shown in Figure 3, first developments

CONFIDENTIAL

This document contains information affecting the national defense of the United States within the meaning of the Espionage Laws, Title 18, U.S.C., Section 793 and 794, the transmission or revelation of which in any manner to an unauthorized person is prohibited by law.

are designed for use with ballistic missile stages. The NOMAD (Pressurized fluorine/hydrazine) and CENTAUR (pump-fed oxygen/hydrogen) programs are currently being actively prosecuted. Another concept which has been evolved as a result of systems cost analyses, designated "Aurora", is exemplified by a pressure-fed upper stage system using an uncooled ablative bell nozzle. The initial stage in development of the Aurora concept is the 15,000 pound thrust HYDRA shown in Figure 5. It is now ready for development to prove-out the concept. Once the concept is proven, it should be applied to subsequent Aurora stages which could be developed in the 30-60 and 100-150,000 pound thrust ranges. These would provide stages applicable for use with high thrust stages which would evolve from either the conventional approach to the Phoenix approach to development.

The demand for maximum performance and versatility in the last stage indicates that present types of propulsion systems, both pressure-fed and pump-fed should be judiciously developed. In the 100-150,000 pound thrust range, pump fed systems would be explored with emphasis on the liquid oxygen-liquid hydrogen propellant combination. Techniques for restart and thrust modulation should be established and sufficient work using all attractive propellant combinations be pursued to determine conclusively their relative merits for system applications as they arise.

The liquid fluorine/liquid hydrogen combination offers the greatest performance potential in chemical propellants. No aggressive program now exists for determining whether this performance is practical of achievement. A program should be pursued at a moderate level to determine the answer to this question and establish the feasibility of pump-fed systems using fluorine. The experimental pump program would also be applicable to stages using fluorine with hydrazine.

No decision times are indicated in Figure 5 as they were for Figure 3. This is because the upper stage program should be broad in scope, under continuous close surveillance, and frequent technical and management decisions will probably be required. Not discussed here in detail, but also required to enable successful accomplishment of military missions by the booster vehicle are broad programs for the development of low thrust vernier maneuvering, and attitude control propulsion systems.

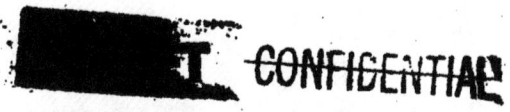 CONFIDENTIAL

This document contains information affecting the national defense of the United States within the meaning of the Espionage Laws, Title 18, U.S.C., Section 793 and 794, the transmission or revelation of which in any manner to an unauthorized person is prohibited by law.

CONFIDENTIAL

CONFIDENTIAL

BODY-90

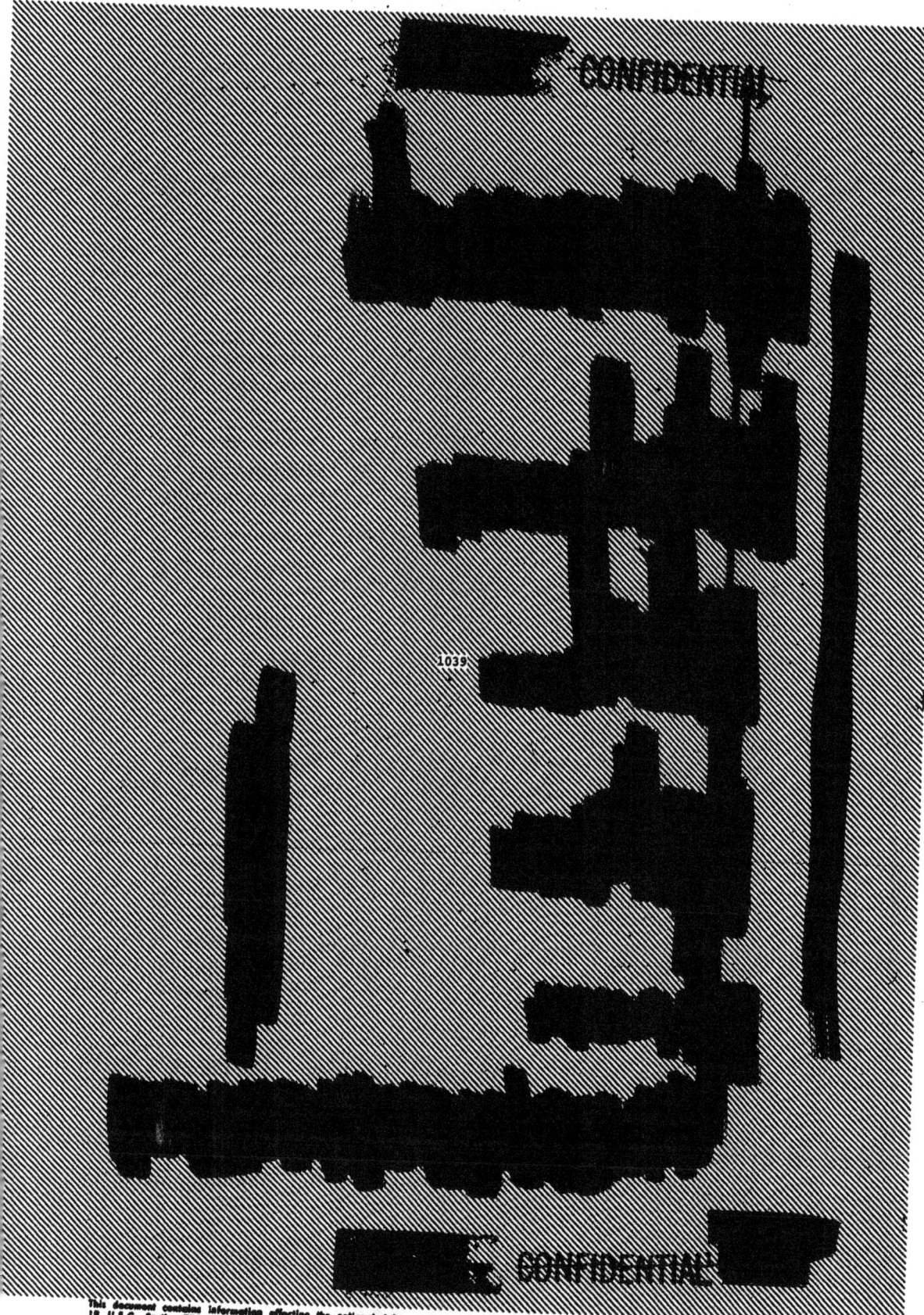

CONFIDENTIAL

CONFIDENTIAL

This document contains information affecting the national defense of the United States within the meaning of the Espionage Laws, Title 18, U.S.C., Section 793 and 794, the transmission or revelation of which in any manner to an unauthorized person is prohibited by law.

CONFIDENTIAL

CONFIDENTIAL

WDZR-160
G-15

18, U.S.C., Section 793 and 794, the transmission or revelation of which in any manner to an unauthorized person is prohibited by law.

CONFIDENTIAL

CONFIDENTIAL

BODY-93

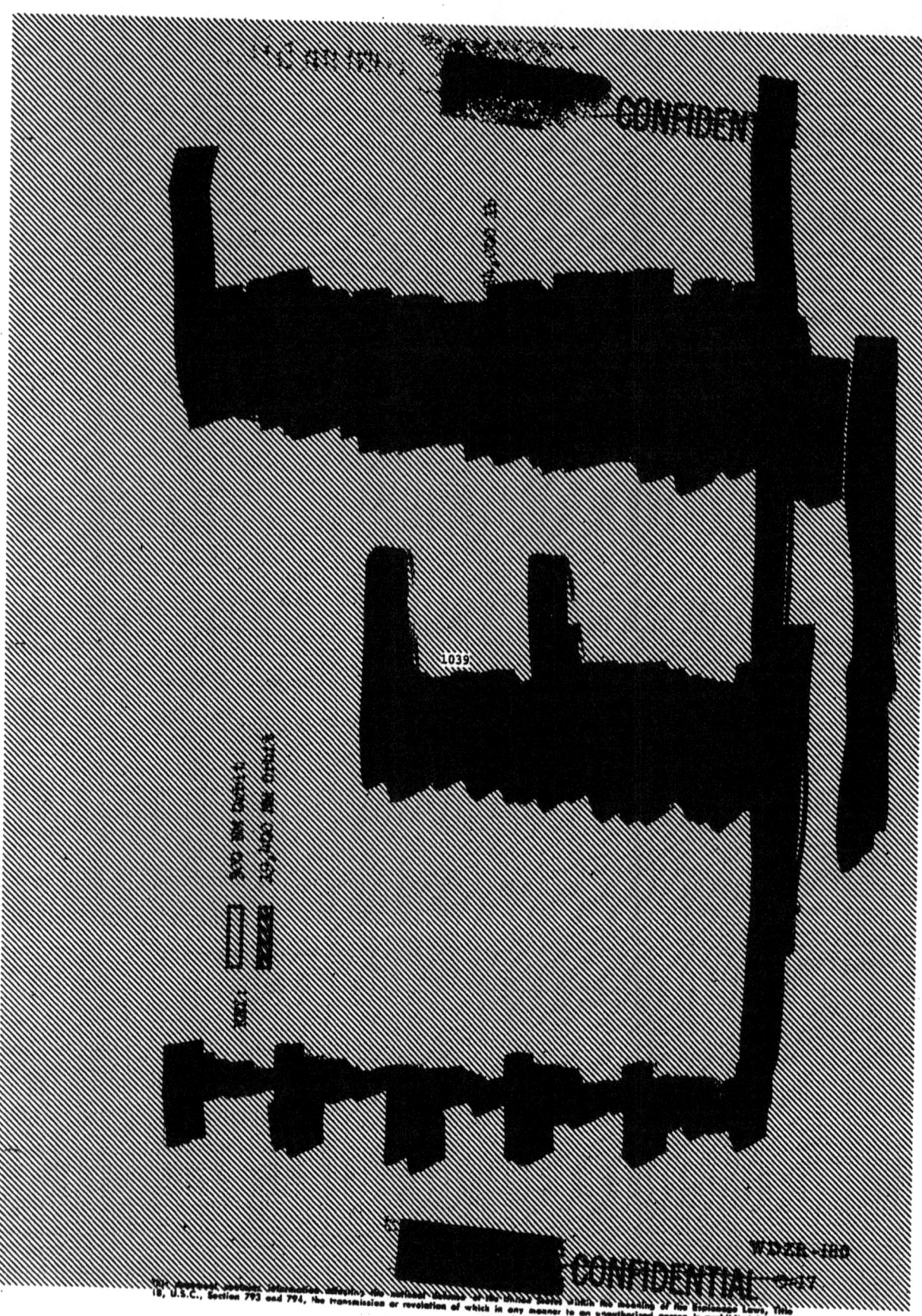

CONFIDENTIAL

1039

CONFIDENTIAL

This document contains information affecting the national defense of the United States within the meaning of the Espionage Laws, Title 18, U.S.C., Section 793 and 794, the transmission or revelation of which in any manner to an unauthorized person is prohibited by law.

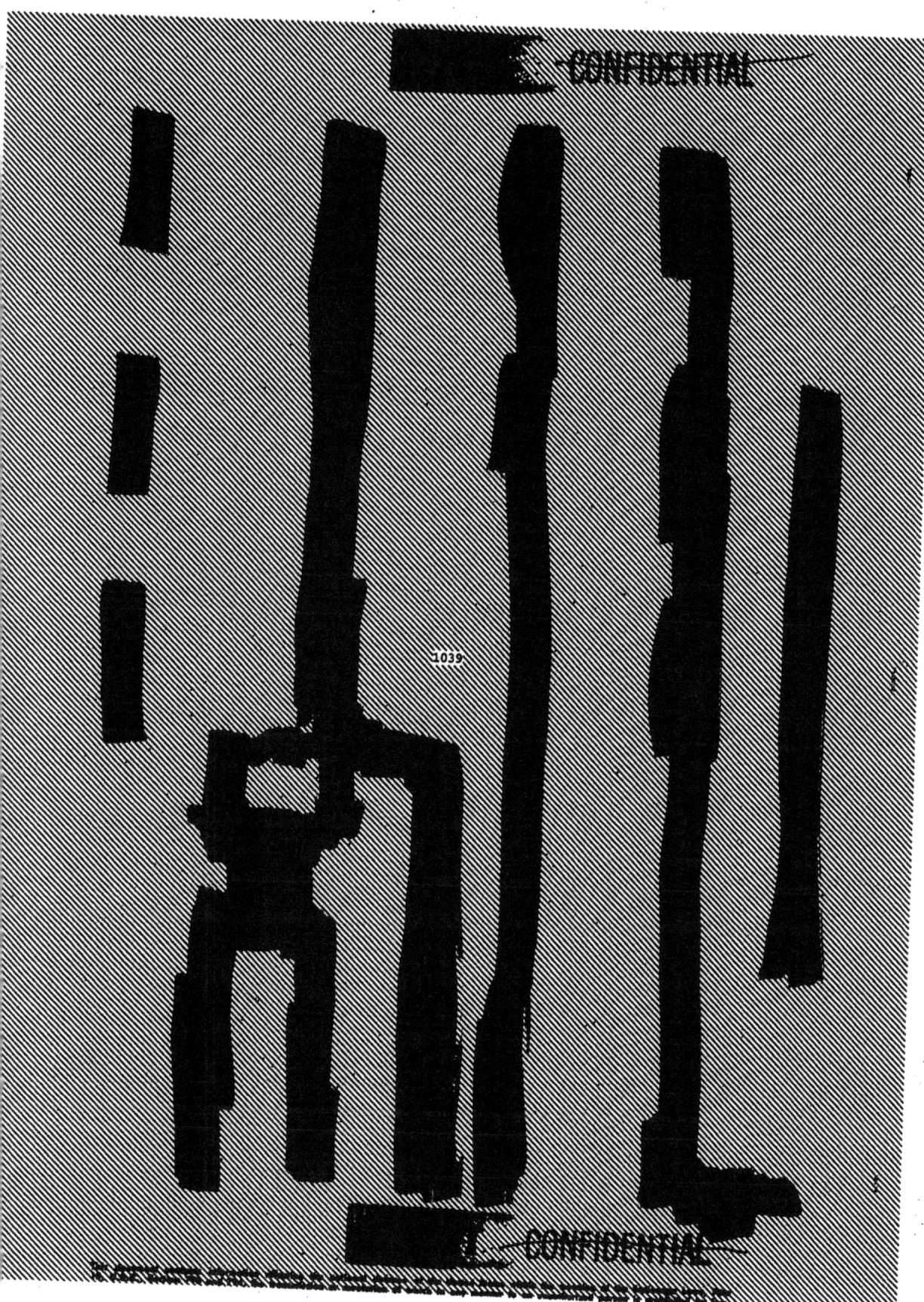

CONFIDENTIAL

CONFIDENTIAL

Appendix D - Representative Research
and Development Areas

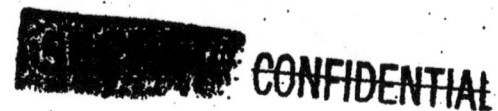

APPENDIX D

REPRESENTATIVE RESEARCH AND DEVELOPMENT AREAS

This section mentions representative development and research areas which are or could support military space systems development. The lists are organized by technical disciplines and should be considered as preliminary information. No effort has been made to indicate a priority or associate the subjects with specific systems development programs. The list is included merely to suggest areas of interest and to stimulate further study and suggestions.

A. Development Programs

The programs represented by the items on the list should be continued or initiated at an early date in order to meet system requirements.

1. Communications and Radar

a. Transmitters

(1) High Power

High-power transmitters and duplexing techniques permitting simultaneous transmission of command and reception of telemetry data, or a single direction antenna, are required. High-power solid-state devices should be developed for high efficiency transmitter amplifiers.

(2) Airborne

High efficiency, light-weight, phase-stable, airborne transmitters with power output of 100 watts or greater are required for long range telemetry and accurate guidance systems.

b. Telemetry and Command

(1) Automatic

Develop automatic telemetry demodulation and recording equipment for digital information; FM telemetry demodulation equipment for extremely noisy signals.

WDZR-180

 CONFIDENTIAL D-1

This document contains information affecting the national defense of the United States within the meaning of the Espionage Laws, Title

 CONFIDENTIAL

(2) <u>Secure Telemetry Transmission</u>

Secure transmission is defined as transmissions which cannot be decoded, even though complete engineering information is available to an enemy interceptor. One example is the use of psuedorandom noise techniques for encoding digital information.

(3) <u>Digital Telemetry and Encoding</u>

Digital telemetry provides a capability for automatic ground data demodulation, recording, and processing. Techniques should be developed for digitizing as wide a variety of data as feasible.

(4) <u>Digital Telemetry Transmission</u>

Digital transmission systems must be developed which provide maximum information rates for given transmitted power level and for given bandwidth of radio signals.

(5) <u>Secure Commands</u>

Secure command transmission systems should be developed.

c. <u>Receivers</u>

(1) <u>Low Noise</u>

Low noise, light-weight, efficient amplifiers are required to provide long range communications with a minimum weight of communications equipment in the vehicle. Maser and parametric amplifier technology should be applied.

(2) <u>Solid-State</u>

Solid-state receivers providing excellent noise figures are urgently needed. These receivers must have minimum power drain so that continuous operation within a satellite is feasible for periods of a year or more.

WDZR-180

 CONFIDENTIAL

D-2

This document contains information affecting the national defense of the United States within the meaning of the Espionage Laws, Title 18, U.S.C., Section 793 and 794, the transmission or revelation of which in any manner to an unauthorized person is prohibited by law.

CONFIDENTIAL

(3) Phase-Lock

Development of improved phase-locked receivers with narrow bandwidths are required in order to receive very weak signals in the presence of noise.

(4) Correlation

Advanced data correlation techniques should be developed for improved communications, radar detection, and security against jamming.

d. Antennas

(1) Large Size

Economical large antennas must be developed. Large antennas are needed for earth satellites to provide wide communications bandwidth with reasonable transmitter power. Such antennas are obviously badly needed for lunar probes, and interplanetary probes as well.

(2) Back Lobe Control

In ground installations the primary beam of the antenna is pointed at a source with a low noise temperature and the back and side lobes are directed to receiving radiation from a source with high noise temperature such as the Earth. Therefore it is necessary to develop antennas which eliminate the back and side lobes as much as possible, in order to take advantage of the low-noise receiver characteristics.

(3) Electronic Scanners

Electronically scanned antennas will relieve the problem of accurately and rapidly positioning very large ground-based antennas.

(4) Position-Seekers

Light-weight, directional, position-seeking antennas

WDZR-180
D-3

CONFIDENTIAL

This document contains information affecting the national defense of the United States within the meaning of the Espionage Laws, Title 18, U.S.C., Section 793 and 794, the transmission or revelation of which in any manner to an unauthorized person is prohibited by law.

are required for use in space vehicles. It is necessary that vehicle antennas be directional in order to have high gain. Because of the directional properties of the antennas, it is necessary that they be self-orienting.

e. Radar Systems

(1) Improvements

Improved radar performance through the development of modifications for existing radars (e.g., FPS-16) are required.

(2) Ground-Based

Ground-based radars capable of detecting space vehicles of 1 square meter at ranges to 30,000 miles (24-hour satellite range), and of accurately tracking them, are needed as sensors for SAINT-type program.

(3) Satellite-Borne

Satellite-borne radars for detection and tracking of other satellites at ranges from 30 miles (for SAINT) and greater require major state-of-the-art advances.

2. Computers and Control

a. Control

(1) Simplified Guidance and Control

Methods of avoiding the use of a stable platform in boosters to obtain simplified guidance and control should be investigated. One possible approach consists of using improved wide-angle body-mounted gyros instead of a platform.

(2) Pneumatic and Hot Gas Servos

Present methods of thrust vector control generally require power servos to accomplish the thrust vectoring Pneumatic servos, particularly those employing hot gas, show promise of increasing system reliability and producing simplification. The development of a hot gas servo system capable of operating directly from gas obtained from missile fuel combustion is desirable.

WDZR-180

 CONFIDENTIAL D-4

This document contains information affecting the national defense of the United States within the meaning of the Espionage Laws, Title 18, U.S.C., Section 793 and 794, the transmission or revelation of which in any manner to an unauthorized person is prohibited by law.

 CONFIDENTIAL

(3) Miniature Inertial Platform for Attitude Reference

Such a platform will be useful for a number of attitude control and orbit correction applications. In particular it will be useful for such reorientation tasks as are beyond the capability of autopilot systems and in which a full inertial guidance system is not required, or in which radio guidance is used.

(4) Hot Gas Sources

Development of an efficient chemical energy source of hot, high pressure gas, for use in attitude control and orbit-keeping of satellites using jet reaction is needed. Present systems using compressed inert gas for this function are unduly heavy and of limited life. The system must be stable, reliable, controllable and instantaneously restartable many times.

b. Operational Flight Safety

A general purpose inertial operational flight safety unit would be applicable to a variety of missions, and will probably be necessary for some.

c. Orbit Control

The development and demonstration of orbit-keeping subsystems for space satellites must proceed as rapidly as possible. This equipment is a vital functional part of any operational system which utilizes a large number of earth satellites whose positions must be maintained precisely. A most common application of the requirement for orbit-keeping is in systems where a large number of satellites are used to provide complete coverage over the surface of the Earth, or a portion of it, for purposes of reconnaissance, surveillance, or communication. An accurate system of position-keeping of the orbit of each satellite will reduce to a minimum the number of satellites necessary to make the over-all system successful. Orbit-keeping equipment is scheduled to be developed in Project TACKLE or Project DECREE of the Communication Satellite Program, and can be

WDZR-180

 CONFIDENTIAL B-5

This document contains information affecting the national defense of the United States within the meaning of the Espionage Laws, Title 18, U.S.C., Section 793 and 794, the transmission or revelation of which in any manner to an unauthorized person is prohibited by law.

expected to be useful in the satellite AICBM program, the Satellite Interceptor Program, the Reconnaissance Satellite Program, the navigation satellite program, Program MIDAS, outer-space weapons testing surveillance systems, weather surveillance systems, and similar satellites. Because of the widespread use anticipated for this type of equipment, and the lack of present experience in its design and system integration, this technology should be developed at a research level at the earliest possible moment.

    d.   Computers

      The following developments in the computer area are applicable to missile and space programs, and should be supported:

    (i)   Thin-film memory computer

    (ii)   Thin-film circuit techniques

    (iii)   Minimum power and weight computers

    (iv)   Minimum power circuits

    (v)   Connectors for compact memories

    (vi)   Phase-logic computing systems (information carried in phase of sine wave)

    (vii)   High-speed elements and microprogramming techniques (minimum number of components)

    (viii) Efficient digitization of data.

3.   Guidance and Tracking

    a.   Inertial Guidance

      (1)   Lightweight System

        A lightweight inertial guidance system is required for injection guidance applications to be used in many of the military space mission programs. Such a unit might also be used with a modestly manueverable re-entry nose cone or lifting vehicle to reduce aerodynamic or MECO error-induced dispersions. It could also be used during lifting

This document contains information affecting the national defense of the United States within the meaning of the Espionage Laws, Title 18, U.S.C., Section 793 and 794, the transmission or revelation of which in any manner to an unauthorized person is prohibited by law.

 CONFIDENTIAL

re-entry to control the impact point or for changing target. The CENTAUR program has such a guidance system development project associated with it, and this should be continued, but the development of a second such system, of somewhat different performance and capability, should be started in 1960. Some study evaluation of subminiature techniques is desirable as a companion to microelectronic computer developments.

b. Radio Guidance

(1) Modulation

There is a requirement for more simple and more reliable modulation and demodulation techniques in order to obtain more accurate guidance. Modulation and demodulation equipment is used in systems which resolve angular ambiguities while operating at signal-to-noise ratios which are less than unity.

(2) Phase Stability

There is a requirement for techniques and equipment with greater phase stability in interferometer systems. The ability to accurately measure angles and angle rates depends on phase stability of the equipment.

(3) Very Stable Oscillators

It is possible to simplify guidance equipment by utilizing very stable oscillators in the vehicles. The use of a very stable oscillator enables Doppler measurements to be made from one way transmission.

(4) Secure Communications Techniques

Secure communications techniques must be developed for incorporation into radio guidance systems. Such techniques are essential if radio guidance is to have a place in military guidance applications. The problems involved are quite difficult, and a great deal of development work is required to resolve them.

WDZR-180

 CONFIDENTIAL -7

This document contains information affecting the national defense of the United States within the meaning of the Espionage Laws, Title 18, U.S.C., Section 793 and 794, the transmission or revelation of which in any manner to an unauthorized person is prohibited by law.

(5) Wide Base Systems

Development of an operational wide base radio guidance system is required if radio guidance accuracy is to be improved by a large factor.

(6) Frequency Conversion

There is a requirement for a small, reliable, lightweight device for performing frequency multiplication and division.

c. Terminal Guidance

The use of terminal guidance enables a vehicle to hit a target when the location of the impact point is not accurately known at the time of launch. Development of accurate terminal guidance systems may help make AICBM and tactical ICBM and IRBM systems possible. The following types of terminal guidance systems should be developed:

(i)   Map matching systems
(ii)   Infrared seeking systems
(iii) Radio frequency seeking systems
(iv)   Other types of terminal guidance systems

d. Tracking

(1) Automatic Steering

Techniques are needed which will accurately steer ground station antennas to the correct azimuth and elevation for a passing satellite, based on the transmission of a few parameters from a central computing center. Such equipment must be economical and simple to be widely used in a number of ground tracking stations. Further, such a computer at each station will reduce the work load on the central computing facility such as the SPAN Center.

(2) Range Instrumentation

As guidance systems become more and more accurate, radio tracking systems to measure guidance system performance must be developed with improved high accuracy.

WDZR-180

This document contains information affecting the national defense of the United States within the meaning of the Espionage Laws, Title 18, U.S.C., Section 793 and 794, the transmission or revelation of which in any manner to an unauthorized person is prohibited by law.

BODY-104

(3) Automatic Search

Equipment for automatic search acquisition and tracking of satellites under conditions of low transmitter power, high angular tracking rates, short transmissions from satellites, or combinations of all three, is required.

(4) Ballistic Camera

An improved ballistic camera capable of tracking from launch through engine cutoff is required for adequate ICBM flight test evaluation. With the current camera, the flashing light carried by the vehicle is obscured by the light from the rocket engine. A camera shutter, synchronized with the flashing light, and with a very short exposure time, is required.

4. Power

Intensive effort should be directed toward development of ultra-lightweight high efficiency electrical power conversion and generation systems for use in space vehicles. Efficient power sources of lifetimes from a month to several years will be needed. Solar cells, fuel cells, and thermal energy converters should be considered.

a. Solar Cell Auxiliary Power Systems

Solar radiation affords an excellent means for providing power aboard satellites which must remain in orbit for long periods of time. There exists an urgent need for reduction in the size, weight, and cost of silicon solar-cell arrays. Novel schemes for orienting solar energy concentrators or large arrays toward the sun must be developed in order to satisfy the increased power requirements of satellites without making excessively large booster vehicles necessary.

b. Electrochemical Batteries

Batteries are used in all missiles and as energy storage devices aboard satellites. It is necessary to continue development and evaluation of various types of batteries to achieve improvements in specific

WDZR-180

D-9

This document contains information affecting the national defense of the United States within the meaning of the Espionage Laws, Title 18, U.S.C., Section 793 and 794, the transmission or revelation of which in any manner to an unauthorized person is prohibited by law.

weight, cycle of life, internal impedance, usable temperature range, shelf life, and packaging. New test techniques to predict performance are needed.

c. Fuel Cells

Certain types of fuel cells show promise of yielding much lower specific weight in applications where electrochemical batteries are now used. A regenerative fuel cell system should be developed capable of gravity-free operation for one year. Maximum output power should be 200 watts after at least 2000 charge-discharge cycles. Nonregenerative fuel cell systems should be developed for one-hour to one-month lifetimes.

d. Rotary Energy Converters

For large but short duration hydraulic and electric loads, turbine driven pumps and electric generators give a system of low specific weight. Continued development of hot gas and solid fuel turbine drives, and novel types of brushless generators, and variable speed-constant frequency generators, is required.

e. Static Converters

Development should be continued on solid-state static inverters and voltage changers in the 1 KW range and above, to yield maximum possible efficiency. Methods of improved radio noise suppression in circuits which use switching devices should also be developed.

5. Propulsion and Vehicles

a. Chemical Booster Systems

(1) Conversion of Present Systems

Convert present ICBM engines (e.g., ATLAS) to $LOX-N_2H_4$ combination for higher payloads and longer range capabilities (interim Big Bang applications).

(2) High Altitude Performance

Develop high altitude performance capabilities for the present ATLAS and TITAN booster engines. This includes high expansion

This document contains information affecting the national defense of the United States within the meaning of the Espionage Laws, Title 18, U.S.C., Section 793 and 794, the transmission or revelation of which in any manner to an unauthorized person is prohibited by law.

ratio nozzles and altitude start and restart capability so that these engines can be used in upper stages for very large boosters.

(3) 400,000 Pound Booster

Develop a LOX-RP booster engine of the 500K thrust level class (such as the Rocketdyne E-2) for use in second generation ICBM's of the Big Bang type, and also in boosters for various Air Force space missions.

(4) Reliability

Develop reliability features in booster engines suitable for manned missions. (Man-engine integration.)

b. High Energy Chemical Systems

(1) Small Engine

Develop small O_2-H_2, pressure-fed engine with uncooled thrust chamber (i.e., Hydra) for general upper stage use (SAINT, Communications Satellite, etc.).

(2) Fluorine

Develop small fluorine stage (in combination with N_2H_4 or possibly H_2) for upper stage ballistic missile applications requiring high energy propellants and more compact envelope than the O_2-H_2 stage.

(3) Medium Engine

Develop medium sized O_2-H_2 pump-fed engine for use as upper stage engines of super booster systems. Basic engine size should be 150K to 200K thrust level.

c. Storable Propellant Systems

(1) Ballistic Missile Applications

Develop small storable propellant engines for use in ICBM systems with greater mobility. These could be N_2O_4-N_2H_4, pressure-fed engines with uncooled thrust chambers. Thrust range would be 10,000 pounds to 30,000 pounds and greater, depending on stage applications.

WDZR-180

 CONFIDENTIAL D-11

This document contains information affecting the national defense of the United States within the meaning of the Espionage Laws, Title 18 U.S.C. Section 793 and 794. the transmission or revelation of which in any manner to an unauthorized person is prohibited by law.

(2) Space Vehicle Applications

Develop a family of small storable rocket engines for various space application--manned and unmanned missions. These engines should have restart, maneuvering, and throttling capabilities. They can be monopropellant or bipropellant storable systems. Thrust range would be anywhere from 50 to 5000 pounds.

(3) Attitude Control System

Develop a monopropellant or bipropellant propulsion system for a lightweight, long-life, quick-response attitude control system.

d. Movable Nozzles

A large effort is currently underway to develop nozzles movable about one axis for the MINUTEMAN system. This effort should be continued, and in addition, nozzles capable of two degrees of freedom should be investigated as a product improvement which may yield a more reliable and lighter-weight system.

e. Vehicles

(1) High-Energy Second Stage

The development of an optimum size second stage rocket using a liquid-hydrogen liquid-oxygen propulsion should be initiated. This development would provide a vehicle stage for use in delivering very large ballistic or orbital payloads in conjunction with the existing ballistic missile boosters. The proposed missile stage utilizes the same propellants as the ATLAS-CENTAUR stage which is under development by NASA. However, it is felt that a stage of greater simplicity and smaller size will provide nearly the same payload and be more adaptable for operational use and space research applications. This objective can be accomplished with a pressure-fed stage which is approximately 50 per cent as large as CENTAUR.

This document contains information affecting the national defense of the United States within the meaning of the Espionage Laws, Title 18, U.S.C., Section 793 and 794, the transmission or revelation of which in any manner to an unauthorized person is prohibited by law.

BODY-108

(2) Recoverable Boosters

The design development and demonstration of recovery systems for large rocket boosters should be initiated as soon as possible. Large payloads require very large rocket propelled boosters to be developed and fabricated in substantial numbers. The high expense of this size of booster can be expected to become a major limiting factor in the magnitude of space mission effort if a new booster is required for each launching. The development of systems for the recovery of the very large first stage boosters can be expected to substantially reduce the cost of the use of very large vehicles, since it is readily recognized that the cost of the actual liquid propellants used in each missile firing is an extremely small portion of the whole cost. It is possible that the recovery of boosters could be accomplished through the use of drag, rocket propulsion energy, air-breathing engines, parachutes, or controllable lift. In general, the technology necessary for the design evaluation of each of the above techniques is fairly well in hand, with the exception of the last technique involving the use of controlled hypersonic lift. Further research and experiment in this area of technology will be required. When this technical information is available the integrated design of a recoverable booster system could be intensively studied. This should then be followed by a development and flight demonstration program.

f. Ground Support

Design studies and conceptions should be developed for launchers and support systems for use with very large chemical rocket boosters. Safety and handling problems associated with the high energy propellants that are expected to be used in the future systems, should also be considered.

g. Large Boosters

Programs, such as SATURN and TITAN C, for the development of large boosters should continue in anticipation of large payload requirements.

WDZR-180
D-13

This document contains information affecting the national defense of the United States within the meaning of the Espionage Laws, Title 18 U.S.C. Section 793 and 794, the transmission or revelation of which in any manner to an unauthorized person is prohibited by law.

BODY-109

6. Sensors

a. Attitude Sensors

(1) Geocentric and Attitude Rate

Of very vital need at the present time are devices used to sense the local vertical and attitude deviation. Accurate reconnaissance, target acquisition, and orbit correction all depend on extremely stable attitude control of satellite vehicles. Instruments currently available are cumbersome devices involving rotating parts and extensive logic circuitry. Equipment using electronic, optical or infrared techniques for horizon sensing should be developed. Of major importance are accuracy and noise level, which should be measured for currently available hardware in the proper environment.

(2) Heliocentric

Heliocentric sensors should be developed in order to orient devices which depend upon solar radiation such as solar energy cells. These sensors may also be useful for navigation purposes. Sensors should be developed at infrared and optical frequencies. Radio frequencies should also be investigated.

(3) Low-Drift Attitude Sensors

An order-of-magnitude reduction in the drift rate of gyroscopes is needed to enable attitude control during long duration missions, by conventional all-inertial means. This could possibly be achieved by basing the development of a gyro on cryogenic, electrostatic, or molecular effects. Other principles such as the effect of body rates on standing waves or vibrating strings should be considered. A further mechanization of a drift-free attitude sensor might consist of using well-known vacuum measurement techniques to determine the relative number of molecular free space particles which are intercepted by two orthogonal surfaces. In this manner, the vehicle attitude relative to its velocity vector can be determined.

This document contains information affecting the national defense of the United States within the meaning of the Espionage Laws, Title 18, U.S.C., Section 793 and 794, the transmission or revelation of which in any manner to an unauthorized person is prohibited by law.

 CONFIDENTIAL

(4) Very Low Rates

One of the more promising methods for determination of very low attitude rates is the stellar drift meter. This device should be evaluated, both as a rate and as an attitude measuring device. In this regard, the techniques of map reading or map matching may prove applicable. Detection of dark satellites by means of relative motion requires techniques similar to those used in measuring stellar drift. Measurement of lateral ground velocity is necessary for certain lunar missions.

(5) Electromagnetic Attitude Measurement

The possibility of determining space vehicle attitude from vehicle electromagnetic radiation patterns has been proposed in several forms. These should be evaluated for possible use for attitude monitoring.

b. Position Sensors

(1) Detection

Devices are required to detect satellites or re-entry vehicles at long ranges, and under a variety of environmental conditions, for satellite interception, warning, and anti-ICBM programs. Radar, radio, infrared, and optical techniques should be considered. Methods of extracting guidance and control signals from such sensing devices need to be developed.

(2) High Resolution

The use of space vehicles to determine the position of ground installations during reconnaissance or early warning missions requires some form of extremely high resolution sensing, and very accurate control of vehicle body rates. The high resolution photography techniques should be investigated, either separately or combined with attitude sensing.

(3) Weather Reconnaissance

Weather satellites will require simple, lightweight, low-resolution sensors and data transmitters for cloud cover reconnaissance.

 CONFIDENTIAL

WDZR-180
D-15

This document contains information affecting the national defense of the United States within the meaning of the Espionage Laws, Title 18, U.S.C., Section 793 and 794, the transmission or revelation of which in any manner to an unauthorized person is prohibited by law.

c. **Acceleration Sensors**

The development of accurate acceleration sensors is required to enable the development of more accurate inertial guidance and navigation systems. For such systems position computations are based upon attitude measurements and acceleration measurements.

d. **Other**

Developments are needed in every type of instrumentation to make devices useful in space applications.

7. **Components, Packaging, and Environmental Test**

a. **Components**

(1) **High Frequency Transistors**

There is a need for high frequency transistors which can operate above 1000 megacycles/second output, from low power levels to power levels of the order of many watts.

(2) **Digital Control System Components**

The use of digital computers for missile control as well as guidance has many advantages. However, complete integration requires a number of digital-analog devices not currently at the required state of development. A transducer which can measure engine angle and provide a direct digital signal is desirable. In addition, a hydraulic or pneumatic valve which accepts a digitally coded signal would simplify the over-all system. Both of these components require development to meet missile system requirements.

(3) **Bearings for Space Environments**

Of particular importance in meeting the space environment is the vacuum bearing problem. At the present time, inadequate information is available regarding the effects of vacuum on bearing surfaces or how to overcome the problems due to lack of lubrication, vacuum soak, and surface sputtering. Life tests on specially designed bearings should be performed in simulated space environments.

WDZR-180

D-16

 CONFIDENTIAL

This document contains information affecting the national defense of the United States within the meaning of the Espionage Laws, Title 18, U.S.C., Section 793 and 794, the transmission or revelation of which in any manner to an unauthorized person is prohibited by law.

(4) Command Controlled Miniature Integrating Accelerometer

A miniature integrating accelerometer unit capable of accepting "start", "reset", and "velocity to be gained" commands is necessary for missions having vehicle stages which do not demand full inertial guidance capability and for which direct radio control of cutoff is inconvenient. Such commands could be generated from the ground or from the previous stage.

b. Packaging

(1) Lightweight Control System

Ultra-lightweight minimum size equipment for guidance and control of space vehicles should be developed. It should have the capabilities of being programmed throughout the vehicle trajectory. It should also have automatic course correction capabilities for use of an astro-navigation device.

(2) Electronic Equipment Microminiaturization

Studies should be conducted to apply microminiaturization to electronic assemblies. This should include the employment of techniques of thin films, single crystals and molecular structures to complete systems of electronic circuitry. This would permit the inclusion of high performance control and data systems in missile and satellite payloads.

(3) Application of Tunnel Diodes

(4) Intergranule Corrosion Control in Aluminum and Magnesium Alloys

(5) Deposition of Thin Films for Plasma Jet Techniques

(6) High Performance Rocket Nozzles Requiring less Rhenium

(7) Ultrasonic Welding Techniques

(8) Methods of Production of Ultra-pure Metals

WDZR-180

 CONFIDENTIAL D-17

This document contains information affecting the national defense of the United States within the meaning of the Espionage Laws, Title 18 U S C Section 793 and 794 the transmission or revelation of which in any manner to an unauthorized person is prohibited by law.

 CONFIDENTIAL

c. Environmental Test

(1) Flight Tests

The effect of rocket launch and space environment on the reliability and performance of specific missile components should be evaluated at every opportunity in order to decrease the failures of these components when subsequently used in system development flight tests. This type of test is suggested as a part of the advanced THOR-ABLE series, but should also be done as "Piggy-Back" tests on ICBM flight tests and new stage development flight tests.

(2) Space Environmental Laboratory

In order to shorten the development time of hardware items for space application, facilities for limited simulation of zero gravity, radiation pressure, meteorite impact, ionization levels, etc., as found in space, would be desirable.

8. Biology

Design, development, and demonstration of various equipment and conceptions necessary to integrate men into the space missions structure is required. It is suggested that present investigations now underway be extended and additional studies be instituted in the area of manned-environmental subsystems, data displays, control system inputs, and mission integration. Special consideration should be given to the function that a man would perform in a missile system and the effect that the availability of man's capabilities might have on the basic design of the missile system. One promising consideration is the very wide range of equipment performance redundancy that can be provided by a man because of the tremendous adaptability of his mental processes.

B. Research Projects

1. Communications

a. Improvements in Channel Capacity

 CONFIDENTIAL

WDZR-180
D-18

This document contains information affecting the national defense of the United States within the meaning of the Espionage Laws, Title 18 U.S.C. Section 793 and 794, the transmission or revelation of which in any manner to an unauthorized person is prohibited by law.

(1) Coding

The capacity of a communication channel to transmit information is affected by received signal power, system bandwidth, and noise level. It is necessary to increase the capacity of communication channels in actual systems to more nearly approach the theoretical limit. Coding is one method of increasing the capacity of a channel. At the present time coding techniques which enable a system to approach the theoretical limit of capability are very complex and unreliable. It is required that these optimum coding techniques be simplified and made more reliable.

(2) Narrow Banding

Research is required in order to extend the state-of-the-art in narrow banding techniques. While still permitting the narrow bandwidth techniques required for low signal to noise, methods must be devised for obtaining fast acquisition as required in guidance, tracking, and communications.

(3) Detection in Noise

Techniques are required for increasing information rates used for communications and telemetry above those presently possible. Present techniques for resolving signals in the presence of noise, limits our information to rates which are less than desired.

(4) Noise

Research is required to obtain other new techniques for improving signal-to-noise ratio.

b. Propagation

(1) Ionosphere

There are many propagation phenomena characteristic of the ionosphere and its tenuous outer extension which are only very imperfectly known at the present time. Work in this field should be pursued vigorously. This is of special importance to guidance systems and communication systems.

WDZR-180
D-19

CONFIDENTIAL

This document contains information affecting the national defense of the United States within the meaning of the Espionage Laws, Title 18 U.S.C., Section 793 and 794, the transmission or revelation of which in any manner to an unauthorized person is prohibited by law.

(2) Troposphere

Continuing research work is required on the propagation phenomena of the troposphere. This region is currently responsible for some of our worst precision radio guidance problems.

(3) Solid and Exotic Propellants

Further research work is required in connection with the effects of the loading of solid propellants with metals such as aluminum and lithium on radio propagation through the missile flame. For example, it would prove embarrassing to discover that a radio guidance system developed for a specific solid propellant vehicle could not be used because of excessive flame attenuation. The same type of problem arises, potentially at least, in connection with exotic liquid fuels.

(4) Radio Scintillations

New radio scintillation data from radio astronomical as well as satellite signals should be subjected to statistical studies, using improved methods of statistical inference. Complementary theoretical studies of e.m. propagation by fluctuating media should be carried out. The over-all objective is to gain improved information about the size, shape, orientation, motions and stability of ionospheric irregularities which cause amplitude and phase scintillations in radio waves, and thereby introduce a natural limit to tracking accuracy.

(5) Plasma

The transmission of high powered signals through weakly ionized plasma is a nonlinear problem which has characteristics quite different from that of weak signals. Strong low frequency signals can modify a plasma such as the missile exhaust so as to reduce blackout and phase shifting. Applications to the powered, as well as re-entry, phase of flight should be investigated. Electromagnetic propagation experiments and actual equipment evaluations can be planned as Piggy-Back experiments on existing rocket firings, as part of a re-entry test vehicle program, and by special rocket firings as required but available in other programs.

WDZR-180
D-20

 CONFIDENTIAL

This document contains information affecting the national defense of the United States within the meaning of the Espionage Laws, Title 18, U.S.C. Section 793 and 794, the transmission or revelation of which in any manner to an unauthorized person is prohibited by law.

 CONFIDENTIAL

(6) V. L. F.

Very low frequency radar cross sections should be evaluated to estimate feasibility of missile detection in the powered phase from magnetically conjugate points on the surface of the earth.   The detailed propagation of V. L. F. through nonisotropic plasma as well as V. L. F. noise background in the upper atmosphere is under investigation and will continue. Since this noise background is directly related to the Van Allen Belt high speed electrons, considerable activity on satellite radiation belt measurements should comprise part of this program.   V. L. F. propagation theory is also extended to frequencies which are less than the gyro frequencies of the protons.

c.   Secure Communications

Secure communications techniques require extensive research work, as there are a number of basic problems outstanding, of which the most difficult is probably the synchronization problem.

2.   Computers and Control

a.   Control

(1)   Thrust Vector Control by Gas Injection

Methods of thurst vector control which require no heavily loaded moving parts are desirable.   One such method, which as yet has not been fully investigated, employs gas injection normal to the thrust cone walls to cause controlled separation with a resultant controlled change in thrust vector direction.   A development of a thrust vectoring system is necessary before the method can be evaluated.

(2)   Adaptive Control

A definite need exists for control systems for ballistic missiles which are truly self-adapting to changes in missile system characteristics and flight environment.   Recent advances in the field of adaptive control theory have promise; however, a need exists for a concentrated effort to determine adaptive control techniques directly applicable to ballistic missile control.   In addition, such techniques may be required for control during a controlled re-entry.

WDZR-180

CONFIDENTIAL   D-21

This document contains information affecting the national defense of the United States within the meaning of the Espionage Laws, Title 18, U.S.C., Section 793 and 794, the transmission or revelation of which in any manner to an unauthorized person is prohibited by law.

 CONFIDENTIAL

(3) Torque Producing Devices

Development of torque producing devices for changing the vehicle attitude is currently centered around reaction wheels and low thrust jets using stored gas, monopropellants, or bipropellant fuels. Larger torque ranges and improvements in dynamic performance are required. Other approaches such as solar sails or magnetic controls should be investigated. For low altitude vehicles, aerodynamic force may prove usable. The investigation of control techniques must of course be closely allied with physical measurements in the space environment.

(4) Nonlinear Control Systems

On-Off (maximum effort) control systems are presently used for roll control during powered flight and for attitude control of space vehicles. However, such nonlinear methods have not been successfully applied to pitch or yaw control of large ballistic missiles during powered flight. It would be highly desirable to investigate methods of control similar to the maximum effort type for the powered flight application. Such methods hold promise of simplification, increased reliability, reduced weight.

(5) Missile Dynamics

The dynamic behavior of ballistic missiles during powered flight is still not completely understood. A need exists for additional study of the dynamics of liquid propelled ballistic missiles where the fuel sloshing frequencies and body bending frequencies are close together.

(6) Sloshing in Free Fall

Requirements for coast period during the powered flight phase introduce problems associated with the behavior of liquid in the fuel tanks during free fall. The dynamic effects of liquid fuel motion during free fall must be determined in order that attitude control systems for the coast period can be designed.

 CONFIDENTIAL

WDZR-180

D-22

This document contains information affecting the national defense of the United States within the meaning of the Espionage Laws, Title 18, U.S.C., Section 793 and 794, the transmission or revelation of which in any manner to an unauthorized person is prohibited by law.

 CONFIDENTIAL

b. Computers

(1) Computer Simplification

The current state-of-the-art requires vast computer facilities for performing relatively simple guidance function in launch, midcourse and terminal phases. It is required that studies be made to determine simple forms of guidance equations for special purpose missions where low information rates are required.

3. Guidance and Tracking

a. Guidance

(1) Sensors

New and more accurate sensors are required for determining position and attitude. Studies should be made to determine more accurate techniques for obtaining data utilizing radio, radar, optical, infrared, and inertial techniques and combinations of these techniques.

(2) Terminal Guidance Techniques

Accurate methods are required for terminal guidance in order to accomplish missions with a high degree of accuracy without placing extremely severe requirements upon launch guidance, midcourse guidance, and propulsion.

(3) Midcourse Guidance Techniques

Accurate midcourse guidance techniques are required in order to accomplish missions requiring a high degree of accuracy without placing an undue burden upon propulsion, launch guidance, and terminal guidance. Studies are required to evaluate the relative advantages of control from the vehicle with control from the ground.

(4) Noninertial Attitude Sensors

Radio Attitude Sensing Systems and other noninertial methods should be studied.

 CONFIDENTIAL

WDZR-180
D-23

This document contains information affecting the national defense of the United States within the meaning of the Espionage Laws, Title

(5) <u>Radio Guidance</u>

Research work is required for highly accurate, wide-base radio guidance systems.

(6) <u>Secure Guidance</u>

Extensive research work is required in secure communications and anti-jamming techniques for effective military radio guidance systems.

(7) <u>Doppler-Inertial Guidance Systems</u>

Careful study of the relative merits of various possible combinations of Doppler and inertial equipment is needed. Among the important criteria are accuracy, reliability, flexibility and cost.

New devices such as cesium-beam and gas-cell frequency references are promising, but considerable theoretical study, exploratory laboratory study, and engineering development are needed. Some components requiring special study are crystal oscillators, spectral lamps, and interaction cells.

Improvements of methods and equipment by which the stability of frequency references can be measured are needed.

An investigation is needed of errors caused by variations of the time of transmission of radio waves through missile flames of various types.

(8) <u>System Simplification</u>

It is required that studies be made to reduce the complexity and weight of guidance systems. In this regard the studies should evaluate the use of simple radio and inertial combinations.

(9) <u>CEP Improvement Research</u>

There is a need for a strong research program to investigate the over-all problem of CEP reduction. In the immediate sense, such programs exist in the various ICBM weapon systems, but there currently exists no long-range program of this nature.

This document contains information affecting the national defense of the United States within the meaning of the Espionage Laws, Title 18, U.S.C., Section 793 and 794, the transmission or revelation of which in any manner to an unauthorized person is prohibited by law.

b. **Tracking**

   (1) **Fast Acquisition**

Research is required to obtain new methods for fast acquisition of targets. With present techniques the acquisition time is inversely proportional to the square of the communications bandwidth. Therefore, as the bandwidth is made narrower to improve the signal-to-noise ratio, the acquisition time increases considerably.

   (2) **Computer Accuracy**

For the purpose of precise determination of orbits it is required that studies be made to obtain more accurate computation programs, especially with regard to integration.

   (3) **Location of Ground Stations**

Accurate tracking of satellites is contingent upon an accurate knowledge of the location of the ground stations which perform the tracking. Studies are required to determine methods of measuring the position of ground stations more accurately through tracking of satellites.

   (4) **Data Reduction**

Studies are required to determine the optimum smoothing of data in order to obtain the best estimate of measured quantities.

   (5) **Secure Tracking**

Research is required to devise techniques for secure tracking systems which are capable of operating in the presence of counter-measures.

c. **Flight Mechanics**

   (1) **Trajectories**

Studies are required to determine methods of trajectory selection for maximum performance. Optimum computation techniques must be devised for selecting pitch programs which consider the constraints of the

WDZR-180

 CONFIDENTIAL D-25

This document contains information affecting the national defense of the United States within the meaning of the Espionage Laws, Title 18, U.S.C., Section 793 and 794, the transmission or revelation of which in any manner to an unauthorized person is prohibited by law.

propulsion system and of vehicle heating. Computational techniques must also be devised to obtain optimum steering in yaw which complies with the range safety and the propulsion system requirements.

(2) Satellite Orbits

The basic properties of satellite orbits must be studied in order to determine precise trajectories. The effects of the various perturbing forces must be known more accurately. Detailed results must be determined for special satellites which require precise orbits.

d. Physics

(1) Re-entry Physics

The optical, infrared, and radio character of the re-entry wake should be established. Its passive appearance (how it looks over the entire frequency range) should be studied. In addition, radio propagation (including the V. L. F. range) aspects should be analyzed. In particular, radar cross sections of the wake for various aspect angles should be estimated.

(2) Geophysics

(a) Determination of geodetic and gravimetric information to greater accuracy for high accuracy systems.

(b) Research on upper atmospheric wind and density fluctuation to be continued for higher accuracy systems.

(c) Geophysical environment parameters should be determined to far better accuracy than now known. For instance, the radiation levels should be known in all portions of space surrounding the Earth, the energy and type of radiation should be known, the effects of solar activity on this radiation may be very important.

(3) Geodetic Requirements

Refined studies of the effects of geopotential fluctuations on long-range trajectories should be carried out.

WDZR-180

D-26

This document contains information affecting the national defense of the United States within the meaning of the Espionage Laws, Title 18, U.S.C., Section 793 and 794, the transmission or revelation of which in any manner to an unauthorized person is prohibited by law.

e.   Propagation

The propagation research mentioned as being necessary for communications in paragraph VII B 1 b is equally applicable to both guidance and tracking.

4.   Power

Research on systems for conversion of solar, heat, or nuclear energy to usable electric power must be stepped up in order to meet the increased electronic requirements of satellites. The following laboratory projects should be initiated.

a.   Photovoltaic Converters

Continue research on semiconductors to improve efficiency and lower cost of solar cells. Investigate novel methods of obtaining p-n junctions in large area devices and fabricate units with multiple junctions. Study photoluminescence as a possible method of energy storage.

b.   Thermionic Conversion

Thermionic diodes have been used successfully for conversion of heat to electric power. Possible efficiencies are higher than those for thermoelectric or photovoltaic conversion. Considerable research is needed to arrive at practical thermal and mechanical designs. The possibility of using grid structures or split anodes for direct conversion to chopped d-c or a-c voltages should definitely be pursued.

c.   Exotic Heat Engines

More advanced heat engines which can provide rotomotive as well as electric power will be required for certain satellite operations. Research on items such as mercury vapor pumps and partial admission turbines should be intensified.

d.   Thermoelectric Conversion

Research on materials which exhibit large thermoelectric effects should continue in support of the design of thermal conversion systems.

WDZR-180

 CONFIDENTIAL D-27

This document contains information affecting the national defense of the United States within the meaning of the Espionage Laws, Title 18, U.S.C., Section 793 and 794, the transmission or revelation of which in any manner to an unauthorized person is prohibited by law.

 CONFIDENTIAL

Basic research must be performed now to ensure that sufficient power can be made available aboard space vehicles so that ionic propulsion or intense electromagnetic countermeasure techniques can be implemented.

5. Propulsion and Vehicles

    a. Thrust Chamber

        (1) Injector Development

Continue basic investigations of combustion stability with storable and nonstorable propellants.

        (2) Nozzle Configurations

Investigate analysis and design of nonconventional nozzles. This should include experimental investigations, if analytical studies show promise. The systems to be considered should include both the Spike or Plug Nozzle and Unconventional Bell Nozzle (with large expansion angles).

        (3) Uncooled Thrust Chambers

Develop uncooled thrust chambers for use in high energy and storable liquid propellant engines; and perform research on novel schemes of designing uncooled thrust chambers. These should include investigation of the heat-sink method of absorbing the heat for the rocket engine nozzle.

    b. Turbopump Systems

        (1) Cavitation Performance

Investigate cavitation performance of pumping systems in various propellants. Develop scaling laws to predict cavitation performance in various propellants from water tests.

        (2) Design Concepts

Analytical studies should be directed towards unconventional, new design concepts for turbopumps.

WDZR-180
D-28
CONFIDENTIAL

This document contains information affecting the national defense of the United States within the meaning of the Espionage Laws, Title 18, U.S.C., Section 793 and 794, the transmission or revelation of which in any manner to an unauthorized person is prohibited by law.

 CONFIDENTIAL

(3) Hydrogen Fuel

Analytical and experimental studies should be made of pumps suitable for large chemical or nuclear propulsion systems using hydrogen fuel. Studies should include investigation of optimum turbopump design (centrifugal, mixed-flow axial or hybrid) from the standpoint of performance, weight, and development time and cost.

c. Integration of Components Into Systems

Development efforts to permit system simplicity and improved reliability through elimination of components, etc., of present propulsion systems.

d. Propellant Research

Investigate storable propellants, high energy propellant additives. This should include calculation for performance of new systems and consider capability of propellants with present and future systems.

e. Solid Propellant Research

(1) Metal Additives

Investigate combustion of metal additives such as aluminum, magnesium, berylium, and lithium in the propellant grain. Studies should include theoretical and experimental investigations.

(2) Solid Propellants

Study solid-liquid hybrid systems--investigate improving the performance and thrust control of present day solid propellant systems by the addition of a liquid oxidizer.

f. Liquid Propellant Research

(1) Investigate catalytic phenomena relating to monopropellant systems.

WDZR-180

D-29

 CONFIDENTIAL

This document contains information affecting the national defense of the United States within the meaning of the Espionage Laws, Title 18, U.S.C., Section 793 and 794, the transmission or revelation of which in any manner to an unauthorized person is prohibited by law.

(2) Investigate the kinetics of dissociation and recombination of free radicals in rocket nozzles. High energy systems, solid propellant systems, and nuclear monopropellant systems should be investigated.

(3) Investigate the physical and chemical properties of the many liquid propellants of interest for advanced, high energy systems.

g. Aero-Thermodynamic Research

(1) Heat Transfer

Heat transfer investigations related to rocket propulsion systems. These include studies necessary to derive basic information on particle phenomena in nozzle flow and ablation phenomena in uncooled thrust chambers.

(2) Radiation Properties

Study the radiation properties of rocket engine exhaust gases in order to determine their effects on infrared and other similar trackers. This is of great importance in SAINT and AICBM missions.

(3) Fluid Mechanics Studies

Perform magnetogasdynamics-theoretical studies relating to the containment and shaping of the flow of high temperature gases. These studies should also consider selected thermoelectric energy conversion devices and the containment of the high temperature nuclear plasma gases, and the study of high temperature fluid dynamics problems associated with the advanced nuclear rocket systems.

h. Advanced Propulsion Devices

(1) Investigate low-thrust ion, plasma, and solar cell devices for velocity and attitude control and orbit-keeping in space.

(2) Design Evaluation Studies

Perform design evaluation studies of large solid propellant engines to assess feasibility and practicability of this type system for various Air Force booster missions.

WDZR-180

This document contains information affecting the national defense of the United States within the meaning of the Espionage Laws, Title 18, U.S.C., Section 793 and 794, the transmission or revelation of which in any manner to an unauthorized person is prohibited by law.

(4) <u>Support Studies</u>

Support studies should be initiated or continued to indicate the areas of application and feasibility of various advanced propulsion systems. They include:

(i) Electric Propulsion Systems
(ii) Plasma Propulsion Systems
(iii) Solar Propulsion Systems
(iv) Other Exotic Systems

(5) <u>Low Thrust Systems</u>

Low thrust chemical propulsion systems for satellite applications are also a promising area for research.

i. <u>Pressurization Systems</u>

Develop a lightweight pressurization system for space vehicle applications. These should have long storage capability and be operable under zero-g conditions.

j. <u>Nuclear Demonstration System</u>

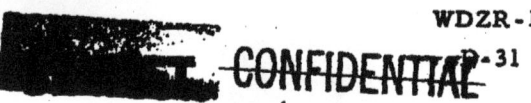

WDZR-180
D-31

CONFIDENTIAL

This document contains information affecting the national defense of the United States within the meaning of the Espionage Laws, Title 18, U.S.C., Section 793 and 794, the transmission or revelation of which in any manner to an unauthorized person is prohibited by law.

k. Decoys

There is a strong requirement on aerodynamics to create a decoy vehicle which will duplicate the radar cross section, the re-entry trajectory, and the same ionized wake as the nose cone. Such a decoy needs to be developed.

l. Communications

Aerodynamic shape choice can greatly affect the problem of terminal trajectory communication through the ionized shock and boundary layers. Techniques and hardware to ease this problem must be developed.

m. Aerodynamics

The studies and tunnel tests of re-entry shapes should continue, especially in the newer fields of maneuverable re-entry.

n. Magnetohydrodynamics

The application of this field to flow problems about the re-entry body requires both analysis and hardware development. Its potentialities are very great.

6. Sensors

A study should be made of exotic, or improved gyroscopic devices and accelerometers. Provisions should be made to exploit any breakthrough in concept, materials, etc. In addition, promising work currently underway should be continued.

7. Structure

a. Weight Reduction

An intensive investigation should be initiated into weight

WDZR-180

This document contains information affecting the national defense of the United States within the meaning of the Espionage Laws, Title 18, U.S.C., Section 793 and 794. the transmission or revelation of which in any manner to an unauthorized ...

SECRET CONFIDENTIAL

saving design techniques. For the foreseeable future, payloads will be weight-limited and a critical examination of standard electronic and mechanical equipment designs should prove extremely valuable. Particular attention should be paid to mechanical joints, webs, and fillets, and to the interface between electrical and mechanical portions of the payload.

    (1) <u>Pressure Vessel Design Criteria Development</u>

Determine material selection and design criteria for high efficiency pressure vessels, including the effects of multi-axial stress fields, stress gradients and discontinuities on the effective strength of high strength materials for pressure vessel applications.

    (2) <u>Development of Design Criteria for Elastic Instability of Thin Shell Structures</u>

Determine the buckling strengths and characteristics of certain stiffened and unstiffened conical and cylindrical shells, including the effects of combined loads and internal pressures.

    (3) <u>Vibrational Characteristics of Solid Propellant Rocket Engines</u>

Determine the structural dynamic interactions of solid propellant case, including the modes and frequencies, effective masses, and damping.

    (4) <u>High Velocity Impact and Penetration Phenomena</u>

Investigate high velocity impact and penetration characteristics of small pellets impacting on various structures.

    (5) <u>Structural Characteristics of Composite Structures</u>

Determine the strength, stiffness, and instability characteristics of layered and composite shell structures under various loading conditions.

    (6) <u>Structural Capabilities of High Strength Alloys</u>

Metallurgical investigation of solute distributions in

WDZR-180

CONFIDENTIAL 33

This document contains information affecting the national defense of the United States within the meaning of the Espionage Laws, Title 18, U.S.C., Section 793 and 794, the transmission or revelation of which in any manner to an unauthorized person is prohibited by law.

SECRET CONFIDENTIAL

high strength alloys, and determination of their relation to the motion of dislocations in the alloy should be performed, in order to understand and exploit the structural capabilities of nominally high strength materials.

(7) Thermal Stresses in Rocket Nozzle Shapes

Measure stresses in the two-dimensional thermal stress field of rocket nozzle structures and correlate with theory.

(8) Shock

(a) Shock Gauge Development

Continue the development of shock gauges for measuring ground shock characteristics.

(b) Ground Shock Characteristics

Physical measurement of ground shock characteristics in various soil conditions for nuclear or high explosive blasts should be performed as a part of hard base site evaluation studies.

(c) Wave Propagation in Non-Linear, Non-Homogeneous, or Layered Media

Experimentally investigate wave propagation characteristics of non-linear, non-homogeneous, or layered media, perhaps including soils, and correlations with theory.

(d) Response of Structures to Excitations by Wave Propagation in Continuous Media

Measure the response of structures contained within or attached to continuous media when excited by waves propagated within the media, and determine the resulting changes in wave propagation characteristics.

(e) Development of Advanced Shock Isolation Systems

Develop methods for shock isolation and protection employing advanced concepts and techniques, perhaps including yielding supports.

SECRET   CONFIDENTIAL

WDZR-180
34

This document contains information affecting the national defense of the United States within the meaning of the Espionage Laws, Title 18, U.S.C., Section 793 and 794, the transmission or revelation of which in any manner to an unauthorized person is prohibited by law.

(9) Sloshing

    (a) Experimental Investigation of Sloshing

        Continue and extend present studies in fluid-sloshing characteristics to understand fluid slosh coupling with flexible tanks, and sloshing control.

8. Components, Packaging and Environmental Test

    a. Space Environment Data

        Space vehicles, either earth-orbiting or probe type, must fly through distrubances arising from a variety of physical phenomena. Among those which are most obvious are solar radiation pressure, gravity gradient effect, and magnetic torques. At the inception of the ballistic missile program, extensive work was conducted to evaluate the wind profile so that missile designers would have a design criteria. A similar effort is now needed to evaluate the physical phenomena which will influence space vehicle design criteria (one of the more important being the effect of these disturbances on attitude control).

    b. Hyper-Environment Investigations

        The effect on the surfacing and thin films of materials as a result of nuclear radiation, ultra-high temperature and combinations of these under vacuum, should be examined.

        This should include examination of the electrical, as well as physical, properties of the materials resulting from high intensity exposure rather than the long duration exposure to these environments.

    c. Valves

        Development of valves for space vehicle applications requires basic research. These components must have long life storage capabilities in space, minimum response time, minimum electrical power consumption, and be capable of operation under zero-g conditions.

This document contains information affecting the national defense of the United States within the meaning of the Espionage Laws, Title 18, U.S.C., Section 793 and 794, the transmission or revelation of which in any manner to an unauthorized person is prohibited by law.

SECRET CONFIDENTIAL

9. Materials

a. Crystals

A fundamental study should be conducted on the properties of crystals and methods of growing large ultra-pure single crystals of organic and inorganic materials under discovering properties useful in electronic equipment design. This is essential for progress in micro-miniaturization.

b. Surface Chemistry

Basic studies of surface chemistry of organic and inorganic materials should be conducted with particular investigation of the electrical properties of their surfaces.

c. Shielding

Lightweight shielding material for protection against nuclear radiation is needed for microminiaturized electronic equipment.

d. Thermochromic

Thermochromic coatings are needed for controlling temperature of space vehicles.

e. "Whiskers"

The properties of fibers and "whiskers" of organic and inorganic materials should be explored in a search for super strength, high heat-resistant flexible materials, leading to reduced weight and high performance of devices in which these could be applied.

f. Propulsion Applications

(i) Investigate the compatibility of materials with various liquid propellants.

(ii) Investigate ablation properties of various materials when used in rocket engine nozzle.

This document contains information affecting the national defense of the United States within the meaning of the Espionage Laws, Title 18, U.S.C., Section 793 and 794, the transmission or revelation of which in any manner to an unauthorized person is prohibited by law.

9. Materials

   a. Crystals

      A fundamental study should be conducted on the properties of crystals and methods of growing large ultra-pure single crystals of organic and inorganic materials under discovering properties useful in electronic equipment design. This is essential for progress in micro-miniaturization.

   b. Surface Chemistry

      Basic studies of surface chemistry of organic and inorganic materials should be conducted with particular investigation of the electrical properties of their surfaces.

   c. Shielding

      Lightweight shielding material for protection against nuclear radiation is needed for microminiaturized electronic equipment.

   d. Thermochromic

      Thermochromic coatings are needed for controlling temperature of space vehicles.

   e. "Whiskers"

      The properties of fibers and "whiskers" of organic and inorganic materials should be explored in a search for super strength, high heat-resistant flexible materials, leading to reduced weight and high performance of devices in which these could be applied.

   f. Propulsion Applications

   (i) Investigate the compatibility of materials with various liquid propellants.
   (ii) Investigate ablation properties of various materials when used in rocket engine nozzle.

CONFIDENTIAL ER-180

D-36

This document contains information affecting the national defense of the United States within the meaning of the Espionage Laws, Title 18, U.S.C., Section 793 and 794, the transmission or revelation of which in any manner to an unauthorized person is prohibited by law.

9. Materials

    a. Crystals

        A fundamental study should be conducted on the properties of crystals and methods of growing large ultra-pure single crystals of organic and inorganic materials under discovering properties useful in electronic equipment design. This is essential for progress in micro-miniaturization.

    b. Surface Chemistry

        Basic studies of surface chemistry of organic and inorganic materials should be conducted with particular investigation of the electrical properties of their surfaces.

    c. Shielding

        Lightweight shielding material for protection against nuclear radiation is needed for microminiaturized electronic equipment.

    d. Thermochromic

        Thermochromic coatings are needed for controlling temperature of space vehicles.

    e. "Whiskers"

        The properties of fibers and "whiskers" of organic and inorganic materials should be explored in a search for super strength, high heat-resistant flexible materials, leading to reduced weight and high performance of devices in which these could be applied.

    f. Propulsion Applications

    (i) Investigate the compatibility of materials with various liquid propellants.
    (ii) Investigate ablation properties of various materials when used in rocket engine nozzle.

WDZR-180

SECRET CONFIDENTIAL

This document contains information affecting the national defense of the United States within the meaning of the Espionage Laws, Title 18, U.S.C., Section 793 and 794, the transmission or revelation of which in any manner to an unauthorized person is prohibited by law.

(iii) Investigate the methods of coating materials with refractories. This information will be directly applicable to problems associated with the development of uncooled thrust chambers.

(iv) Investigate material properties at cryogenic (hydrogen) temperatures and also at the very high temperatures associated with high energy chemical systems and nuclear systems.

(v) Investigate nuclear radiation effects on rocket engine components and propellants.

g. Materials for Cryogenic Applications

Conduct mechanical strength and ductility investigations at temperatures below 100°K to provide information for low-temperature applications.

h. Material Surface Property Requirements for Space Environment

Investigate emissivity and absorbtivity throughout the spectral region as a function of surface conditions; stability of such surface characteristics in the space environment.

i. Physical Properties of Materials for High Temperature Applications

Determine refractory, ablative, sublimative, insulation and strength properties of advanced alloys and non-metallics to meet the strength, thermal shock, and erosion requirements of manned re-entry, propulsion, and other extreme temperature applications.

j. Kinetics of Solid State Transformations

Determine the kinetics of crystal structure transformations in superconductors, semiconductors, intermetallics, and metals to provide increased capabilities of materials in specific present applications and develop improved materials for future applications.

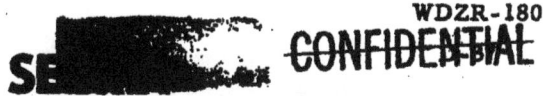 WDZR-180 CONFIDENTIAL

This document contains information affecting the national defense of the United States within the meaning of the Espionage Laws, Title 18, U.S.C., Section 793 and 794, the transmission or revelation of which in any manner to an unauthorized person is prohibited by law.

k. **Radiation Effects in Solids**

Investigate the effect of high energy particle radiation on the useful life of semiconductors and solar cells, as well as development of improved radiation detectors and nuclear auxiliary power supplies.

l. **Physical Properties of Materials in Space Environment**

Determine the effects of space environment, including high vacuum and radiation, on strength and other physical properties of structural materials in an attempt to determine their most effective use in the space environment.

WDZR-180

CONFIDENTIAL

This document contains information affecting the national defense of the United States within the meaning of the Espionage Laws, Title 18, U.S.C., Section 793 and 794, the transmission or revelation of which in any manner to an unauthorized person is prohibited by law.

Printed in the USA
~PSIA information can be obtained
ʷ ICGtesting.com
ᵃˡ30150324
ᵃ009B/113

9 781608 882526